WORKBENCHES

T0243328

Build the Ideal Bench

The Taunton Press

THE TAUNTON PRESS, INC.
63 South Main Street
Newtown, CT 06470-2344
E-mail: tp@taunton.com

EDITOR: CHRISTINA GLENNON
INDEXER: HEIDI BLOUGH
JACKET/COVER DESIGN: BARBARA COTTINGHAM
INTERIOR DESIGN: CAROL SINGER
LAYOUT: SUSAN LAMPE-WILSON

Fine Woodworking® is a trademark of The Taunton Press, Inc., registered in the U.S. Patent and Trademark Office.

The following names/manufacturers appearing in *Workbenches* are trademarks: Benchcrafted©, Craigslist©, Festool©, Gramercy Tools©, Hamilton Marine©, iVAC©, Jorgensen©, Lee Valley©, Lie-Nielsen©, Masonite©, Minwax©, Oneida Dust Deputy©, Veritas©, Woodcraft©, Woodriver©.

Library of Congress Control Number: 2022917981

Printed in the United States of America
10 9 8 7 6 5 4 3 2 1

ABOUT YOUR SAFETY: Working wood is inherently dangerous. Using hand or power tools improperly or ignoring safety practices can lead to permanent injury or even death. Don't try to perform operations you learn about here (or elsewhere) unless you're certain they are safe for you. If something about an operation doesn't feel right, don't do it. Look for another way. We want you to enjoy the craft, so please keep safety foremost in your mind whenever you're in the shop.

DEDICATION

Special thanks to the authors, editors, art directors, copy editors, and other staff members of *Fine Woodworking* who contributed to the development of the chapters in this book.

Contents

INTRODUCTION   2

PART ONE
Workbenches That Work
- Build Your First Workbench   **4**
- Small, Stable Workbench   **10**
- Sturdy, Knock-Down Workbench   **20**
- Simple and Solid Workbench   **31**
- Build a Stout Workbench   **39**
- Shaker Workbench   **52**
- Modified Roubo Is the Ultimate Workbench   **62**
- Outfeed Table Doubles as a Workbench   **74**

PART TWO
Improving A Work Bench
- Don't Build a New Workbench   **84**
- Rethinking the Workbench   **92**
- Work at the Right Height   **100**
- Under-Bench Tool Storage   **104**

PART THREE
Specialized Workbenches
- Minibench Works Wonders   **113**
- The Wired Workbench   **119**
- A Saw Bench Is a Versatile Addition to Your Shop   **129**

PART FOUR

Holding the Work

• 6 Essential Bench Jigs   **137**

• Extra Help for Holding Work   **146**

• Make Short Work of Small Parts   **152**

• Get a Grip on Your Work   **158**

• Clever Clamping Tricks   **164**

• Shopmade "Bench Puppies"   **171**

• The Versatile Wedge   **176**

• All-in-One Workstation for Dovetails   **184**

• A Shooting Board that Handles 5 Jobs   **195**

• 4 Bench Jigs for Handplanes   **202**

• Making Sense of Vises   **209**

Metric Equivalents   **216**

Contributors   **217**

Credits   **218**

Index   **219**

Introduction

Even though I spend a lot of time using woodworking machinery, I still consider the workbench to be at the heart of my shop. It's where I get to slow down, pick up the hand tools I really want to be using, and do the work that elevates the things I make to a level beyond that which I can achieve using power tools alone.

I've gone through a few bench designs during my career, and you probably will too. The first reason is that as a new woodworker, you most likely don't have the tools or skills necessary to build that dream workbench you may have in mind. Even if it's something you want to attempt right away, I'd advise against it. Yes, you need a workbench to accomplish many of the tasks the craft demands, but it shouldn't present a stumbling block to doing the work you want to be doing. Because of that, I'd recommend choosing a design that won't break your budget, and just as important, is something that you can build with a limited skill set and tool collection. We've included a couple of options that will get you up and working quickly and are sturdy enough to serve you well in the long run.

Even with a serviceable bench in your shop, there still may be some reasons to upgrade at some point. A big reason, and one directly related to holding off on your dream bench for a while, is that as a new woodworker, you may not yet have an idea of the type of work you eventually want to do. Once you do find that path, the work may dictate a different sort of bench than the one you originally had in mind. You may also find that as your shop space changes over time, you have the space for a bigger bench, or conversely, you may need something smaller to fit a tighter space. For that reason, we've also included some benches that are worth the time and effort to make once you are up for it, as well as some designs that are at home in smaller shops as well.

In addition, we've also included some great ideas for bench accessories that will let you get the most from your bench. With these in hand, you'll be ready to tackle a variety of tasks that you may not have even thought possible. With this collection of articles from *Fine Woodworking* in hand, I'm confident that you'll have what you need to begin your woodworking journey with a simple bench, or to step up and build the dream bench you've had in mind for a while.

—Michael Pekovich
    Editor and Creative Director,
    Fine Woodworking

Build Your First Workbench

BOB VAN DYKE

Aworkbench with an end vise and front vise is easily the most important tool in your shop, one that you use on every project. If you don't already have one, or if yours is old and rickety, it's time to upgrade.

You could just buy a bench—there are some good ones out there—but you could easily spend $1,000 and not improve on the bench I'll show you how to build here for around $300.

This bench is everything a good workbench should be: It is heavy and strong, so it won't skate or wobble. It has a flat surface big enough to support a medium case side or tabletop. And it's capable of holding your work securely, with an end vise that can be used with benchdogs to hold work flat or like a front vise to clamp work upright. Best of all, you can make this bench in a weekend, to your own dimensions, and you don't need a ton of tools.

If you're wondering whether a bench like this can really do the job, I have more

Easy dadoes on the tablesaw. You don't need a dado set to cut the joints on this bench. You'll do it with your standard blade and miter gauge. First the fence gets set. The rip fence will be your stop. Lay out one of the legs and set the fence so the blade lines up with one end of the dado.

Then the fence stays put. Use a spacer block (left) to reposition the leg for cutting the dado's opposite end. Cut each wall cleanly, supporting the leg with the miter gauge, and then make passes to remove the material between them (right).

than 25 of these benches in my school and they are still going strong after 11 years and 3,500 students.

Simple joinery and fasteners make a sturdy base

I like to make the base from ash, maple, poplar, or oak. The base consists of two end assemblies, each built from a pair of crosspieces dadoed into the legs. These

end assemblies are connected by two long stretchers bolted in place on each side. The top long stretchers are rabbeted into the tops of the legs.

All of this joinery is best cut on the table-saw with a dado set but it's also possible, if more tedious, to do the work with a standard blade and a miter gauge. Either way, a single fence setting and a spacer block is used to cut each corresponding joint exactly the same

Workbench in a Weekend

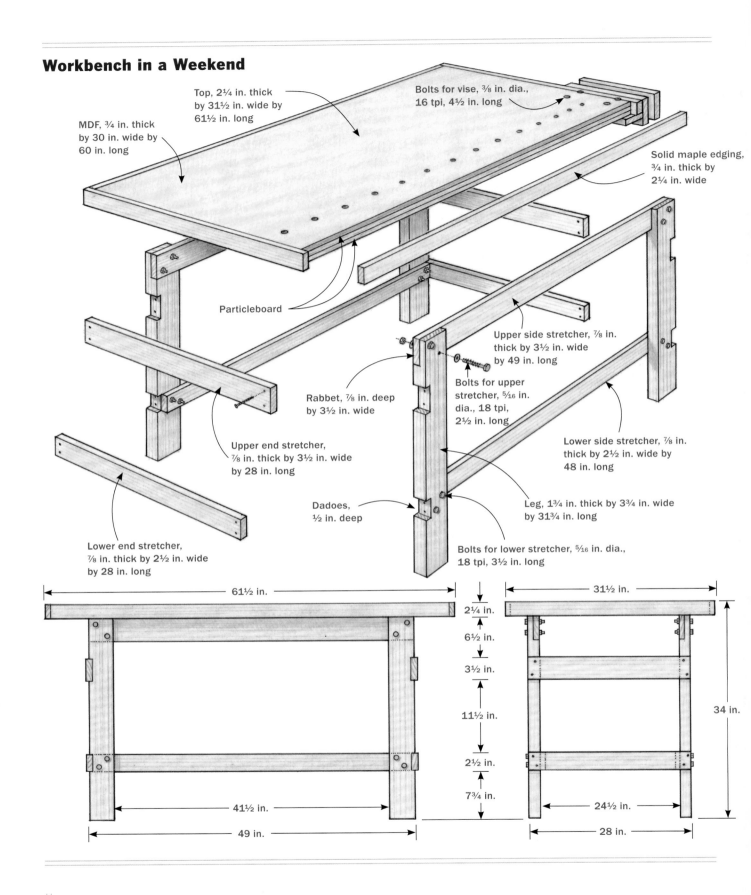

Top, 2¼ in. thick by 31½ in. wide by 61½ in. long

MDF, ¾ in. thick by 30 in. wide by 60 in. long

Bolts for vise, ⅜ in. dia., 16 tpi, 4½ in. long

Solid maple edging, ¾ in. thick by 2¼ in. wide

Particleboard

Rabbet, ⅞ in. deep by 3½ in. wide

Upper side stretcher, ⅞ in. thick by 3½ in. wide by 49 in. long

Bolts for upper stretcher, 5/16 in. dia., 18 tpi, 2½ in. long

Lower side stretcher, ⅞ in. thick by 2½ in. wide by 48 in. long

Upper end stretcher, ⅞ in. thick by 3½ in. wide by 28 in. long

Dadoes, ½ in. deep

Leg, 1¾ in. thick by 3¾ in. wide by 31¾ in. long

Lower end stretcher, ⅞ in. thick by 2½ in. wide by 28 in. long

Bolts for lower stretcher, 5/16 in. dia., 18 tpi, 3½ in. long

61½ in.

31½ in.

2¼ in.

6½ in.

3½ in.

11½ in.

2½ in.

7¾ in.

34 in.

41½ in.

49 in.

24½ in.

28 in.

width and in exactly the same place on each leg. If you leave the crosspieces and stretchers a bit wide, you can edge-plane them in the thickness planer for a precise fit in the dadoes and rabbets.

With the joinery cut, begin construction of the base with the two end assemblies. Before starting, break all the edges with a chamfer or roundover. Check for square during glue-up by measuring diagonally across the assembly in each direction. Adjust at the corners if needed until the measurements match.

The rest of the assembly consists of connecting the two ends by attaching the long stretchers. Set the base upside down on a level work surface and clamp the stretchers in place while drilling the bolt holes. With the base assembled, you can turn it over and use it to build the top.

The top: A triple-decker sandwich

Cutting 4x8 sheets of medium-density fiberboard (MDF) and particleboard by yourself is no picnic. Buy one sheet of each and have your supplier rough them down so each piece is 1 in. bigger than final size in each direction. You can use the particleboard offcuts to piece together the top's middle layer. If you plan your cuts carefully, the middle layer will consist of two pieces with only one seam.

Before assembly, use a tablesaw or a router and straightedge to cut the top layer accurately to final size. Cut the other layers about ¼ in. to ⅜ in. bigger than this layer.

Start the glue-up with the top layer facedown on the base. Roll yellow glue onto the surface, then place the pieces of the middle layer on the waiting piece. Make sure the middle layer extends beyond the top on all sides, then screw them together. Make sure you don't drive any screws where you plan to drill

Build the base first. Glue and screw the end assemblies. Drill pilot holes and countersink for the screws while the assembly is dry-fit (top). Clamp the side stretchers in place when drilling their bolt holes (above).

dog holes. Afterward, use a router and a flush-trimming bit to bring the middle layer flush with the top. Finish the glue-up by repeating the entire process to attach the bottom layer.

Cut the stock for the solid-wood edging no more than ⅛ in. wider than the thickness

1. Trim, then trim again. To assemble the top start with one layer cut to exact size, then use a router and flush-trimming bit to trim the adjacent layers.

2. Add the edging. Use biscuits to align it. Van Dyke uses a shim to offset the biscuit joiner when cutting the slots in the top's edge. This ensures the edging will stand proud of the top for trimming flush.

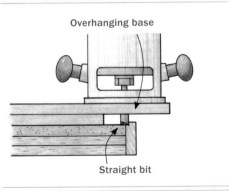

Overhanging base

Straight bit

Trim the edging with a router. This simple base allows a straight cutting bit to trim the edging flush with the surface of the top.

of the top, with each piece about 1 in. longer than its finished length. When gluing the edging to the sides, use thick clamping cauls to distribute the pressure evenly. After gluing the edging in place (long sides first) and trimming the ends, use a router to flush-trim the protruding edging to the core—top and bottom. Then switch bits and round over all the edges. Now is also a good time to sand the benchtop.

3. Outfit with dogholes and a vise. Sighting along an upright square (above) helps in drilling a straight dog hole. When you attach the vise (right), add a spacer block to keep the jaws even with the tabletop.

A single vise does double duty

This bench has one vise, which acts as both a front vise and an end vise. You can use it to hold your work vertically for any sawing or chiseling task or you can use it in conjunction with benchdogs to easily hold a board flat on the benchtop.

Before installing the vise, I use an inexpensive ¾-in. spade bit to drill a row of holes in the top for the benchdogs. I start the row 5 in. from the vise end of the bench and space them about 4 in. apart, but the spacing can vary according to your needs. What is important is that the holes line up with the dog in the vise.

To mount the vise, first make a spacer to fit between the vise and the bottom of the benchtop. It should be slightly longer and wider than the vise's footprint, and thick enough to drop the cast-iron jaws about ½ in. below the top. Hardwood jaw pads go on

before installation, then get planed flush with the benchtop.

Glue and screw the block to the underside of the bench and then clamp the vise in its final position. Mark the location of the vise bolt holes on the bottom of the bench, then use an adjustable square to transfer the locations to the top.

Drilling from the top, start with a Forstner bit to counterbore each hole deep enough to fully recess the bolt head and washer. Use the center dimple left by the bit to drill the through-holes, and bolt the vise in place.

The last thing to do is attach the top to the base. I use six small angle irons available from any hardware store and screw them in (turn the bench upside down).

For a tough, water-resistant finish, I use four coats of Minwax High Gloss Polyurethane on the top and bottom. The finish is exceptionally durable, and can be renewed easily by scuff-sanding with 220-grit sandpaper and brushing on a new coat.

Small, Stable Workbench

MATT KENNEY

All in the joints. Compact design gets its strength and rigidity from clever interlocking joinery.

When we received this workbench proposal from Eric Tan, it was quickly accepted by the *Fine Woodworking* staff. Tan, who specializes in Ming dynasty furniture, incorporated interlocking joinery—a signature detail of that era—into the bench, creating a strong, rigid construction without the need for glue or hardware. The unique design is brilliant, a no-brainer for a shop project.

But there was a problem: For the vast majority of articles, one of our editors travels to the author's shop to take photographs. Tan lives in Taiwan, and I did my best—on several occasions—to convince my editor to send me there to photograph him making the bench. Alas, due to expense and time constraints, my arguments did not prevail. So, instead of flying to Taiwan, I drove a few miles down the road to the shop of Kelly Dunton, who agreed to help us show readers how to make the bench.

Aside from working in imperial rather than metric units of measurement, Dunton made the bench exactly as Tan designed it. There is more to this bench than its ingenious self-locking joinery. When assembled, it's rigid and heavy, making it well suited for handwork like planing, sawing, and chopping mortises. It's also compact, making it perfect for anyone with limited shop space.

A dizzying bunch of mortises

All the joinery was done with a hollow-chisel mortiser and tablesaw. This bench has 28 mortises, ranging from dead-simple to fairly complex, combining a stopped mortise with a smaller through-mortise. Fortunately, none of them are difficult to cut.

Joinery, Not Glue, Holds This Bench Together

Interlocking joints borrowed from Ming dynasty furniture eliminate the need for glue. We chose ash—heavy and strong—for this bench.

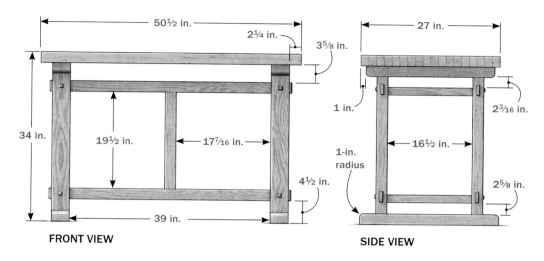

50½ in.

2¼ in.

3⅝ in.

34 in.

19½ in.

17⁷⁄₁₆ in.

4½ in.

39 in.

FRONT VIEW

27 in.

1 in.

2³⁄₁₆ in.

16½ in.

1-in. radius

2⅝ in.

SIDE VIEW

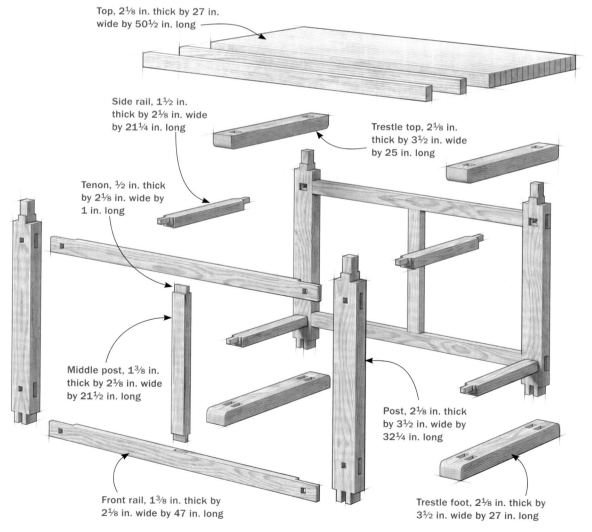

Top, 2⅛ in. thick by 27 in. wide by 50½ in. long

Side rail, 1½ in. thick by 2⅛ in. wide by 21¼ in. long

Trestle top, 2⅛ in. thick by 3½ in. wide by 25 in. long

Tenon, ½ in. thick by 2⅛ in. wide by 1 in. long

Middle post, 1⅜ in. thick by 2⅛ in. wide by 21½ in. long

Post, 2⅛ in. thick by 3½ in. wide by 32¼ in. long

Front rail, 1⅜ in. thick by 2⅛ in. wide by 47 in. long

Trestle foot, 2⅛ in. thick by 3½ in. wide by 27 in. long

Post and Foot are Double-Jointed

Two tenons are stronger and resist racking better than a single tenon. Fortunately, cutting a double mortise-and-tenon isn't much harder than cutting a single one.

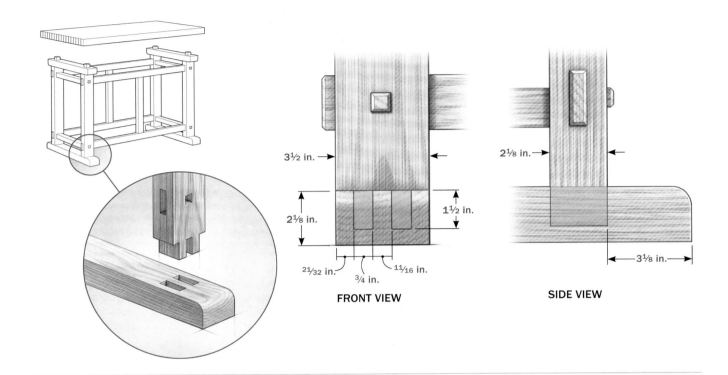

3½ in.

2⅛ in.

2⅛ in.

1½ in.

2¹/₃₂ in.

¾ in.

1¹/₁₆ in.

FRONT VIEW

2⅛ in.

3⅛ in.

SIDE VIEW

After milling the parts to their final dimensions, go to work on the mortises, starting with the most straightforward: those that connect the middle post to the front and back rails. Dunton cut them in two passes with a ¼-in. bit. Set the mortiser's fence to cut the inside wall first, then flip the stretcher around and cut the second wall without moving the fence.

The posts are attached to the trestle feet with double tenons. Dunton used a ⅜-in. bit for these (and all of the remaining mortises). Set the fence for the outside walls of the mortises. Cut the first pair, then flip the foot around to cut the outside wall for the second pair of mortises. Adjust the fence for the inside wall and repeat the process.

Double setup. For the foot's double mortise, set the fence to cut the outside wall. Spin the foot, and do the same for the second mortise. Repeat the process for the inside wall, as shown.

One blade for the cheeks and shoulders. Use a blade that cuts a flat-bottom kerf. For perfectly centered tenons, cut one outside cheek, rotate the post, and cut the other. Adjust the fence and cut both inside cheeks (left). Then shift the fence to nibble away the waste between them. Replace the tenoning jig with a miter gauge and cut the shoulders. A stop block ensures they are aligned (below).

The joint that connects the posts to the trestle tops is a bit more complex. The mortise in the trestle top has a large, rectangular stopped section and a smaller, square through section. Begin with the through-mortise, cutting in from the top to just over 1⅛ in. deep. Flip the trestle top over to cut the rectangular section and connect it to the square portion. Each post has two pairs of intersecting mortises that connect the front and side rails. Cut the stepped mortise for the side rail first. It consists of a larger stopped mortise and a small through-mortise. Again, start with the through-mortise, cutting in from the outside face. Then flip the post and cut the stopped mortise from the inside face. Next cut the through-mortises for the front and back rails. Because of the post's thickness, you'll need to come in from one face and then flip the post and complete the mortise from the other side.

The last four mortises are in the underside of the top, but you can't cut them until you've cut the post tenons and assembled the base. All of the tenons are cut at the tablesaw. Start with the simple tenons in the posts and front

Stepped Tenon Does Twice the Work

The tenon on the top of the post extends through the trestle top and into the benchtop.
The lower part acts as a shoulder for the upper tenon, creating a stronger joint.

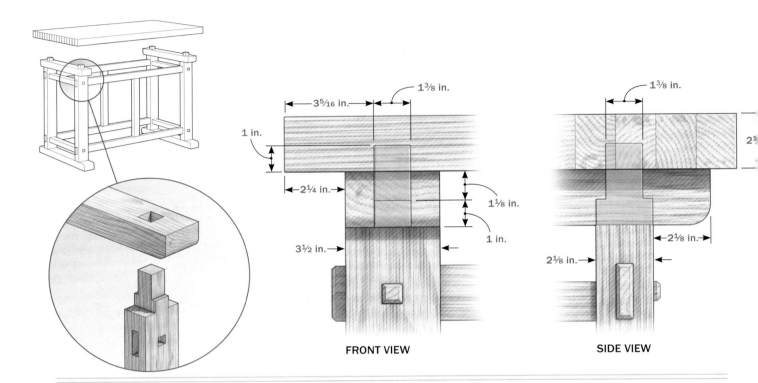

FRONT VIEW

SIDE VIEW

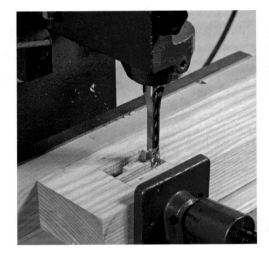

Two mortises in one. First cut the smaller
through-mortise from the other side. Then cut the
larger, stepped one on the underside.

Cut the mating tenon with a dado set. With
the blades set to cut the tenon's small shoulders,
remove waste from the front and back of the post
(above right). Then raise the dado set and cut the
long, thin tenon (right).

and back rails, using a dado set and miter gauge. Cut the tenons in the side rails and the top of the posts. Cut the biggest part of the tenon first, then raise the dado blade and cut the smaller part.

To cut the double tenon at the bottom of the post, use a blade that cuts a flat-bottom kerf, like a rip blade. Using a tenoning jig, cut the two outside cheeks: Cut one of them, flip the post in the jig, and then cut the second.

Rails Lock Together

The tenons on the side rails pass through the tenon on the front rails, tying the posts to the rails.

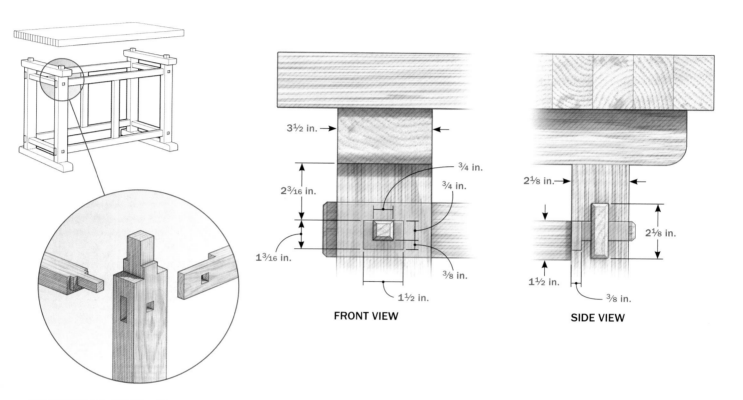

FRONT VIEW

SIDE VIEW

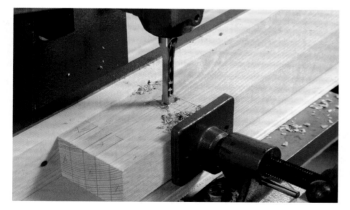

Start with the side rail mortise. Cut the through-mortise from the outside face first, then cut the larger, stopped mortise on the inside.

Then cut one for the front rail. Turn the post on edge and cut halfway through. Flip the post and complete the mortise from the other edge.

Side rail tenon is less complicated than it looks. Start with the large, lower section, cutting the sides and bottom of the rail to create the three shoulders (above). Raise the blade and cut the thin top half (right).

A second setup gets you both inside cheeks, using the same cut, flip, cut process. Nibble out the waste between the inside cheeks by adjusting the jig between cuts so that you work across the waste.

After all of the tenons have been cut, it's time to mortise the tenons in the front and back rails to accommodate the tenon on the side rail. This creates an interlocking joint. Fit one front or back rail tenon at a time. When it's snug in its mortise, lay the post and rail down, so that the mortise for the side rail is facing up. Use a Forstner bit to drill through the tenon where it intersects the mortise. Square up the corners with a chisel. Pull out the rail and move on to the next tenon. After all of the tenons have been mortised, clean up all of the parts, getting them ready for a finish. After this, you can assemble the base.

Dry-fit the side rail. Because the tenon is shaped like a half-lap, make adjustments by planing the side of the tenon with no shoulder.

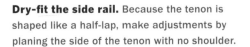

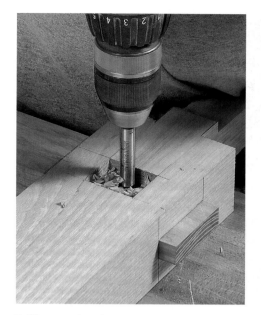

Drill a mortise through the tenon. Use a Forstner bit to remove the waste (left), and then square up the corners with a chisel (right).

A glue-up with no glue

As you put the base together, each new joint assembly locks the previous joint together, so there is only one way to assemble it. Begin by assembling the middle post and the top and bottom front rails. Next, connect the posts to the front rails. The middle post is now locked in place. Repeat this process to assemble the back of the base.

Next, lay down the front assembly and install the four side rails. The tenons on the side rails pass through the tenons on the front rails, locking the posts to the front rails. Lower the back assembly onto the side rails. Now, turn the base upright and lower it onto the feet. Drop the trestle tops into place to complete the base.

Next up is the top. Start with wide boards, ripping them into narrow strips. Flip the strips on edge and glue them together to create the top. This creates a strong top from rift- and quartersawn boards.

Now it's time to mortise the top for the legs. You'll use a template, router, and

Bench Assembles without Glue and Clamps

The interlocking joinery requires a specific order of assembly. Once you settle the top onto the base, all the joints will lock tight.

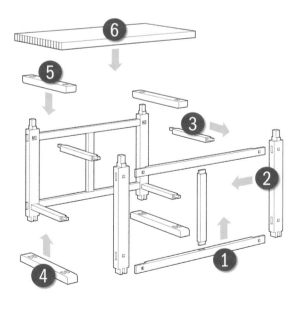

Start with the middle post. It fits between the front rails and adds rigidity to the base. Once you put the posts in place, the front rails are locked to the middle post.

Slide in the side rails. The tenon runs through the front rail and the post, which prevents the post from coming loose from the front rail.

Lower the back onto the side rails. Rest the back assembly on the ends of the tenons and then adjust each tenon until all four are in their mortises. Then the back should slide down (left). The trestle top and foot are next (above)—they lock the posts in place. Now the base is a rigid, single unit.

straight bits for this. Turn the top upside down and put the base on it. The template is made up of three pieces of MDF that are set around the tenon and then clamped in place. Remove the base and you have a perfectly sized template for the mortise. With a spiral bit in your router, remove most of the waste from the mortise, taking care not to rout into the template. Now use a flush-trimming bit to clean up the mortise, following the template. Finally, square up the corners, using the template as a chisel guide. Repeat this process for the other three tenons.

After the mortises are done, turn the base upright and put the top on it. You now have a rigid bench ready for work.

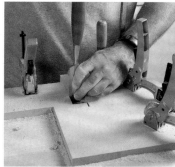

Make a mortising template around the tenons. Working one mortise at a time, Dunton used three pieces of MDF, one of them with a notched corner, to build the router template in place, guaranteeing that the mortise would be located accurately.

Rout the waste. Dunton first used a plunging spiral bit freehand to remove most of the waste, then came back with a pattern bit to flush the sides to the template (top). When squaring the corners (above), the template serves as a guide for the chisel.

A Vise is Optional

A cast-iron vise is a good, proven choice. You'll need to add an apron to the front edge of the top and a spacer block.

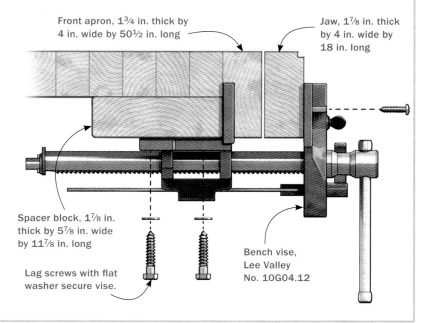

Front apron, 1³/₄ in. thick by 4 in. wide by 50½ in. long

Jaw, 1⁷/₈ in. thick by 4 in. wide by 18 in. long

Spacer block, 1⁷/₈ in. thick by 5⁷/₈ in. wide by 11⁷/₈ in. long

Lag screws with flat washer secure vise.

Bench vise, Lee Valley No. 10G04.12

Sturdy, Knock-Down Workbench

BARRY NM DIMA

When designing this bench, I pulled on old clichés: big, beefy, bombproof, versatile, stout, smart workholding. I shamelessly took from what came before, especially the Moravian workbench and its angled legs. But I wanted something heartier, so I turned to Roubo benches for proportions. Timber framing then lent a hand with the big knockdown joint. The result is a heavy, portable bench that works so well because, at its core, it's so unoriginal. I even took the top from my old bench.

This chapter will focus on building the base and vise. The base's thick parts are built up by laminating two pieces of 8/4 stock

Through-mortise easy in laminated legs. Dowels keep the legs aligned from layout to glue-up. The two halves of the laminated leg get mirroring through-joinery. Dima routs these parts separately, and uses dowels in each half to keep the parts from slipping during layout and assembly.

Lay out the through-mortise on an edge before bringing it across an inside face. The joint lines are square on the edges but have two different angles on the inside. When laying out the edge, clamp the leg halves together to close any gaps.

Saw the ends using a saw guide. To saw accurately, Dima clamps a block along his angled layout lines and presses the saw against that block, which has a jointed edge and face. He uses an azebiki, but a Western saw would work as well.

Bash out most of the waste. Dima kerfs the joint before using a mallet and chisel. He works in from both edges to avoid blowout.

Built in Layers

By laminating the parts, you get a bench that's plenty heavy without buying expensive thick stock. Plus, it takes much of the headache out of the large-scale joinery.

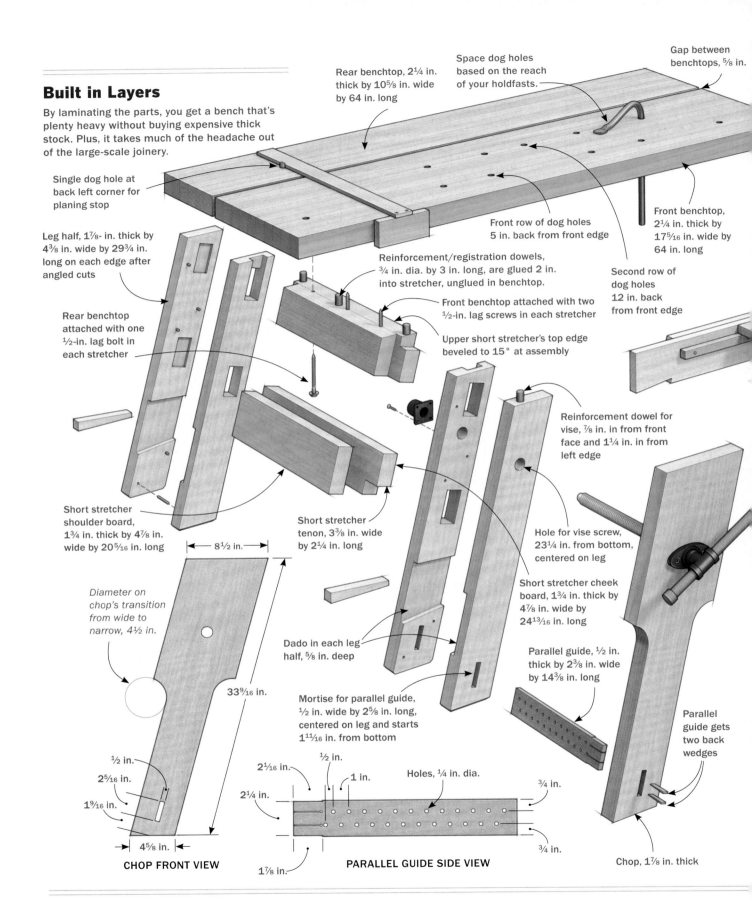

Rear benchtop, $2\frac{1}{4}$ in. thick by $10\frac{5}{8}$ in. wide by 64 in. long

Space dog holes based on the reach of your holdfasts.

Gap between benchtops, $\frac{5}{8}$ in.

Single dog hole at back left corner for planing stop

Leg half, $1\frac{7}{8}$- in. thick by $4\frac{3}{8}$ in. wide by $29\frac{3}{4}$ in. long on each edge after angled cuts

Rear benchtop attached with one $\frac{1}{2}$-in. lag bolt in each stretcher

Front row of dog holes 5 in. back from front edge

Front benchtop, $2\frac{1}{4}$ in. thick by $17\frac{5}{16}$ in. wide by 64 in. long

Reinforcement/registration dowels, $\frac{3}{4}$ in. dia. by 3 in. long, are glued 2 in. into stretcher, unglued in benchtop.

Front benchtop attached with two $\frac{1}{2}$-in. lag screws in each stretcher

Second row of dog holes 12 in. back from front edge

Upper short stretcher's top edge beveled to 15° at assembly

Reinforcement dowel for vise, $\frac{7}{8}$ in. in from front face and $1\frac{1}{4}$ in. in from left edge

Short stretcher shoulder board, $1\frac{3}{4}$ in. thick by $4\frac{7}{8}$ in. wide by $20\frac{5}{16}$ in. long

Short stretcher tenon, $3\frac{3}{8}$ in. wide by $2\frac{1}{4}$ in. long

Hole for vise screw, $23\frac{1}{4}$ in. from bottom, centered on leg

Short stretcher cheek board, $1\frac{3}{4}$ in. thick by $4\frac{7}{8}$ in. wide by $24\frac{13}{16}$ in. long

Diameter on chop's transition from wide to narrow, $4\frac{1}{2}$ in.

Dado in each leg half, $\frac{5}{8}$ in. deep

Mortise for parallel guide, $\frac{1}{2}$ in. wide by $2\frac{5}{8}$ in. long, centered on leg and starts $1\frac{11}{16}$ in. from bottom

Parallel guide, $\frac{1}{2}$ in. thick by $2\frac{3}{8}$ in. wide by $14\frac{3}{8}$ in. long

Parallel guide gets two back wedges

$8\frac{1}{2}$ in.

$33\frac{9}{16}$ in.

$\frac{1}{2}$ in.

$2\frac{5}{16}$ in.

$1\frac{9}{16}$ in.

$4\frac{5}{8}$ in.

CHOP FRONT VIEW

$2\frac{1}{16}$ in.

$2\frac{1}{4}$ in.

$\frac{1}{2}$ in.

1 in.

Holes, $\frac{1}{4}$ in. dia.

$\frac{3}{4}$ in.

$\frac{3}{4}$ in.

$1\frac{7}{8}$ in.

PARALLEL GUIDE SIDE VIEW

Chop, $1\frac{7}{8}$ in. thick

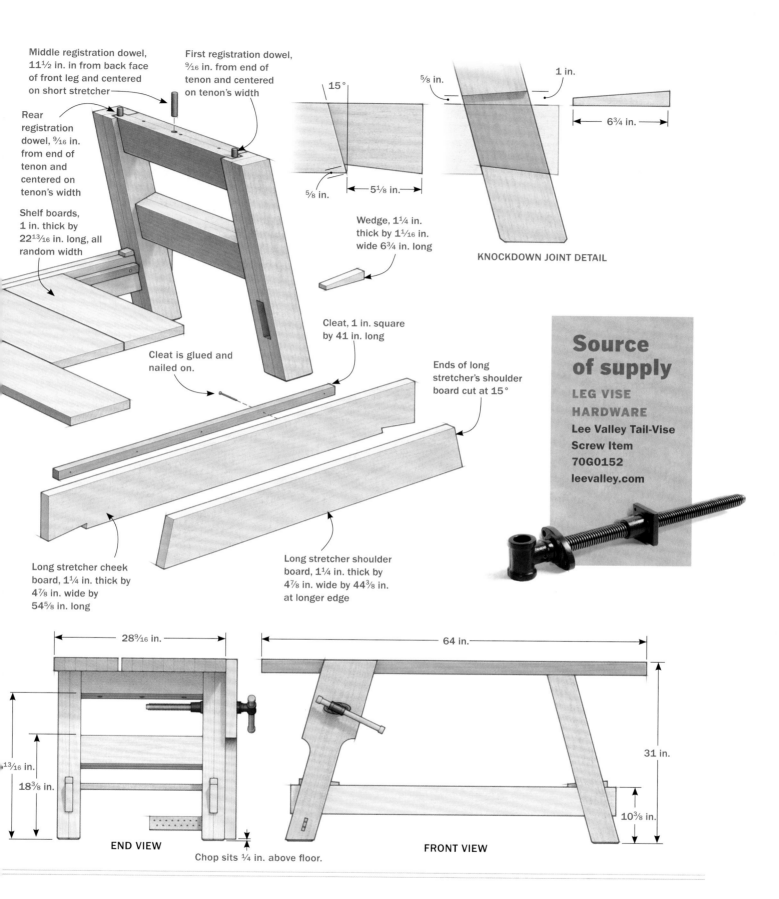

Middle registration dowel, 11½ in. in from back face of front leg and centered on short stretcher

First registration dowel, 9/16 in. from end of tenon and centered on tenon's width

Rear registration dowel, 9/16 in. from end of tenon and centered on tenon's width

Shelf boards, 1 in. thick by 22¹³/16 in. long, all random width

Cleat is glued and nailed on.

Cleat, 1 in. square by 41 in. long

Ends of long stretcher's shoulder board cut at 15°

15°

5/8 in.

5⅛ in.

5/8 in.

1 in.

6¾ in.

Wedge, 1¼ in. thick by 1¹/16 in. wide 6¾ in. long

KNOCKDOWN JOINT DETAIL

Long stretcher cheek board, 1¼ in. thick by 4⅞ in. wide by 54⅝ in. long

Long stretcher shoulder board, 1¼ in. thick by 4⅞ in. wide by 44⅜ in. at longer edge

Source of supply

LEG VISE HARDWARE

Lee Valley Tail-Vise Screw Item 70G0152 leevalley.com

28⁹/16 in.

64 in.

31 in.

⁹¹³/16 in.

18⅜ in.

10⅜ in.

END VIEW

Chop sits ¼ in. above floor.

FRONT VIEW

Rout the joint to depth with a short pattern bit. The bit's bearing lets you clean up the joint's floor without going past the sawn ends. Because the joint is wide, Dima mounts his router on a long auxiliary base.

milled as little as possible. The benefit of this lamination isn't just the lower cost and extra weight, but easy mortise-and-tenons as well, removing some of the pain of working thick parts and adding efficiency instead. The top is just a top, so I won't spill much more ink on that.

Wood selection

The lumber species are all over the place—white pine, oak, ash, and cherry—but with reason. First, much of it was free, so the price was right. But even if I had bought all the boards, they're common, affordable North American domestics, so my wallet wouldn't have taken a huge hit. Then there's the second, more important reason: The parts straddle the line between

workability and weight. The mortised members are pine, while two thirds of what gets tenoned—an easier process—is heavier oak or ash.

Well, the cherry vise chop may not straddle that line. That board was a perfectly sized offcut from a coworker. Without that serendipity, cherry feels a little premium. But it sure does look nice.

To keep the parts as heavy as possible, I kept milling minimal. As long as my glue surfaces were good, I didn't stress about roughness elsewhere.

Laminated joinery

Cutting joinery in parts this large can prove tricky, if not unsafe. This is where lamination comes in; it let me shape each half of the glue-up to create the joinery.

Take the tenons on the short stretchers: Each rear board in the lamination is the cheeks, and each front board creates the shoulders. The result is huge, fast, bareface tenons. Just be sure to cut all the front boards—the shoulders—to the exact same lengths. Otherwise, the shoulder-to-shoulder dimensions will be off, and your assemblies won't be square.

First, though, make the legs. Each gets three mortises, two stopped ones for the short stretchers and one through-mortise for the long stretcher. Here's another benefit of lamination: Instead of cutting this big, deep through-joint in solid stock, you can just form it in each half before glue-up.

To start, clamp the halves together. Then drill for and install alignment dowels. Doing this when the halves are clamped together guarantees the dowel holes line up. Next, lay out the through-mortises on an edge. The dowels make sure the legs go back together exactly as they are now, letting you pull apart the halves to complete the layout.

Keep the dowels clear of this joint, and don't glue them in until you glue up the leg halves. They'll get in the way of the router's long auxiliary base when cutting the mortise.

Despite the angles, the layout's simple provided you make a full-size drawing of the joint. The bottom angle corresponds to the rise-over-run of the long stretcher's dovetail. What that angle is, I have no idea, so I use the drawing to set my bevel gauge. The top angle needs to match the wedge's taper.

Glue up the legs. There is a lot of glue surface, so use plenty of clamps. Be judicious with the glue to avoid squeeze-out, especially in the mortise.

Cut the legs' stopped mortises and saw their angled ends. The stopped mortises are wide and deep, so Dima removes most of the waste with a drill press or plunge router before squaring up their ends with a chisel. The legs' ends, angled 15°, are then cut carefully with a handsaw.

Finish the end assemblies. Cut the short stretcher's tenons to width. These stretchers are also laminations. The shorter front board forms the tenons' shoulders, and the longer rear board forms the cheeks.

After cutting the mating dadoes that create these through-mortises, glue up the legs. Next, cut the stopped mortises. Bore for the vise screw and mortise for the parallel guide. I cut this mortise with a little play in its length so the parallel guide won't get hung up in use.

I then cut the legs to length at 15° top and bottom. Angling the legs means you'll need to bevel the top edge of the upper stretcher too. Before gluing up the end assemblies, drill holes in the upper stretcher for the bolts that will secure the top.

Knockdown long stretchers

The long stretchers, with their half-dovetailed tenons wedged in place, make this bench easily portable, yet the half tail and wedge form a secure, rigid, full dovetail that locks the bench in place. Unlike tusk tenons, which exert pressure against a tenon's end grain, these wedges press against its edge

Dry-fit end assembly to mark the angle on the upper short stretcher. This waste is removed so the stretcher's upper edge lies flush with the legs. Bandsaw close to the line and, after gluing up the assembly, refine the cut with a long plane.

Long stretcher's cheek board gets a half tail on the bottom. Dima keeps the cheek board long so this cut is easier to start. He trims it to length afterward. These stretchers also use laminations to form the tenon.

Assemble the bench's base. After putting the long stretchers into one end assembly, lift and shimmy them into the other end. Seat the joints with a heavy mallet. Chamfers on the feet help prevent splitting at this stage.

Fit and install the wedges. These wedges lock the dovetailed long stretchers in place. Leave them long at this point so there's plenty of room for adjustment. When they fit nicely, trim them to length.

Add the top. The top's front edge is flush with the front faces of the legs. The top itself is two pieces with a ⅝-in. split between.

Dowels register the top on the base, and lag screws keep it there. Install two dowels by the leg vise. These are insurance against the leg vise pushing the top away from the legs. Half-inch lag screws lock down the top.

Leg vises are easy. Install the parallel guide and vise screw in the chop. After drilling the holes in the guide, glue and wedge it into the chop. The vise screw mounts to the chop via standard wood screws.

grain. I can smack them into place without fear of blowing out the mortise.

Like the short stretchers, the long ones are laminated. After cutting the angled ends on the shoulder board, glue it to the cheek board. I cut the cheek board to length only after cutting the half tail. This is for two reasons. First, it takes the stress out of the glue-up, because if the shoulder board shifts along its length, I don't worry about losing necessary tenon length. Second, it's tricky to start a cut on a corner, and an overlong tenon

spares me that. In thickness, these tenons should fit like a slightly subpar glue joint.

The front long stretcher should be flush with the front faces of the front legs. The top's front edge will sit in the same plane, yielding plenty of clamping surface. So, this joint is worth checking with a long straight-edge after assembling the bench. Now's also a good time to nail on the cleats that support the shelf boards, which for me are just random-width scraps from the build, the ugly stuff that didn't make the cut. Finally, drill for the registration dowels that locate the top on the base.

Put the chop, parallel guide, and vise screw in place to locate the vise flange. Don't try to find this location by measuring. Instead, slide the chop against the bench and thread on the flange. When the flange seats flush against the leg, screw it in place.

Leg vise

The vise needs five things to work: a chop, a parallel guide, a screw, a flange, and a handle.

To lay out the chop, I draw a centerline and the 15° bottom end. Almost all other layout comes from these two marks. Cut and shape the chop accordingly, but leave it long at the top for now.

The parallel guide, next, has two jobs. First, it prevents the chop from spinning as you tighten and loosen the screw. Second, it lets the chop pivot against a pin to pinch the work. This is what all those holes are about: You can easily pick the one that lets the chop pivot in to clamp at the top.

The penultimate step is installing the hardware. I use an antique set in the pictures, but modern versions are readily available. Finish up by cinching the chop against the bench to mark its length.

Mark the chop to length. By tracing the length off the top, you're guaranteed to have a chop that matches your bench. Dima saws the piece along the pencil line, letting the chop sit slightly below the benchtop, keeping it out of the way.

Leg vise pivots against pin in parallel guide to pinch workpiece at the top. To secure work in the vise, Dima inserts a drift pin in a hole just beyond the dimension he wants to clamp. He then tightens the vise screw with the workpiece in place. The chop should be slightly farther from the bench at the bottom than at the top, where it needs to pinch the stock.

A tidbit on the top

OK, I will spill some ink on the top, but mainly to emphasize that you should build it to your taste. For example, the split top is nice for storing chisels, saws, and other tools, and it provides purchase for shorter clamps when I clamp something wide to the benchtop's front edge. But it's also a space for shavings and tools to fall into, and it allows the two tops to move independently. To be honest, I'm a little split on it myself.

Then there are the dog holes. I originally drilled mine to work around the repurposed top's old base, and the locations work just as well on this one. The drawing on p. 22 places them where I would. Or just drill yours as you need them. That's cool too.

Simple and Solid Workbench

MASON MCBRIEN

It's hard to do good work without a good bench. But I want to spend my time designing and building furniture, not workbenches, so I like one that's quick to build without sacrificing quality. My go-to for this comes from the Center for Furniture Craftsmanship, where I used to teach. These student benches are no-nonsense affairs that, in some cases, have stood up under decades of considerable use. They not only work well but are a breeze to make, use inexpensive materials that are easy to get, and can be sized to fit nearly any space.

Stripped down bench is all you need

All parts are plywood and ¾ in. thick unless otherwise noted.

Top, MDF, ¾ in. thick by 31⅜ in. wide by 78 in. long

Top bracing, 5 in. wide by 23⅞ in. long

Shelf board, 12¹¹⁄₁₆ in. wide by 72 in. long

Hardwood glue block, 1⅝ in. square

Side apron, 5 in. wide by 23⅞ in. long

8 in.

Narrow leg, 4¼ in. wide at top and 2¼ in. wide at bottom, 31¼ in. long

Long stretcher, 4 in. wide by 72 in. long

Shelf bracing, 4 in. wide by 23⅞ in. long

Legs' taper starts 5¾ in. from top.

Wide leg, 5 in. wide at top and 3 in. wide at bottom, 31¼ in. long

#20 biscuits

The base is made with common birch plywood, although cheaper CDX plywood would work just as well. You don't have to include the shelf down below, but adding it makes this bench nearly bombproof. The top is ¾-in. MDF, which is more durable than you might think. When I was at the school, some benches still had their original tops. Still, if yours wears out over time, it can be replaced easily.

As a bonus, the form is also quite versatile. At the school, some benches had melamine

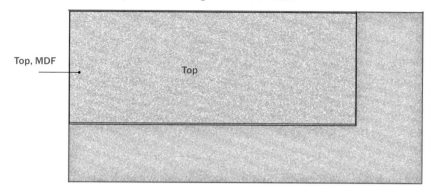

THREE SHEETS MAX
By lining up parts of similar width and length, McBrien expedites breaking down the sheets.

Top, MDF

Top

Base, ¾-in. plywood

Straightedge			
Long apron		Side apron	
Long apron		Side apron	
Top bracing	Top bracing	Top bracing	Top bracing
Wide leg	Wide leg		Wide leg
Wide leg		Extra	
Narrow leg	Narrow leg		Narrow leg
Narrow leg		Extra	
Extra			

Shelf, ¾-in. plywood

Shelf board		Extra
Shelf board		Extra
Long stretcher		Side stretcher
Long stretcher		Side stretcher
Shelf bracing	Shelf bracing	Shelf bracing	Shelf bracing
Extra		

tops and were used for drafting, finishing, layout, and vacuum pressing. Some had insert plates that turned them into router tables. Shrink the design, and you have a sharpening station. I'm making a full-size workbench here, but the design is a blank canvas, so feel free to adapt it however you see fit.

Rigid plywood base

For a workbench this size, the base comes from two sheets of plywood. When I break down the plywood, I start by laying it on a large piece of rigid foam on the floor and use a circular saw. Running a full-size sheet through the tablesaw can be tricky and starting on the floor makes the process easier.

You can cut the benchtop to size this way too. And if you don't have a tablesaw or bandsaw, you can batch out all your parts this way. Later, the foam serves as a flat work surface, letting me assemble the bench without needing another bench—a common problem with other bench designs.

To keep things simple, many components on this bench share dimensions. But each leg is a two-part assembly biscuited and glued together into an L shape. Because they're made out of ¾-in. plywood, one side piece is ¾ in. narrower than the other so the two look even when assembled. I like to taper the legs, too, giving me more foot room when I'm working at the bench.

Don't skimp on the width of the parts, by the way; the wide parts give the bench lots of resistance against racking. Also, the upper bracing goes a long way to stabilize the top and prevent sagging. In my experience, these benches are often stouter than traditional workbenches.

No-nonsense top

Although the top is simply a single layer of ¾-in. MDF, it performs excellently for almost all common woodworking tasks.

Breaking down plywood. For safety, McBrien starts on the floor with a circular saw when cutting a full sheet of plywood. He clamps a second sheet to the one he's cutting and uses the second's factory edge to rip a straightedge, which he'll use as a fence for the next cuts (above). He supports the sheets with a layer of rigid foam.

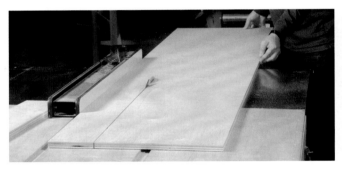

Rips at the tablesaw. When he has manageable sizes, McBrien finishes ripping parts to width at the tablesaw. Since these pieces are still long, he uses infeed support.

Crosscuts at the miter saw. Don't fret about how clean a cut your saw leaves. The ends of these boards will be hidden when the bench is finished.

With its bracing and glue blocks, the surface becomes incredibly rigid—a necessity for efficient pounding and hammering. Its 3-in. overhang all around gives plenty of purchase for clamps.

At the end of the build, I break the benchtop's sharp edges with a rasp for comfort. Then, to protect the MDF from liquids and moisture, I add two or three coats of oil-based urethane.

Vises add versatility

Like the bench itself, the two vises I use deliver great functionality at low cost. While you can get away without one, I recommend adding a front vise to open up workholding options. You don't need anything fancy, although a quick-release mechanism is handy.

BASE

Assemble in stages. Biscuit the leg assemblies. After tapering, the two sides of the leg assemblies are glued together. Biscuits help with alignment and strength.

Use tapered offcut as a caul during glue-up. Clamping tapered parts, like these legs, can be tricky. Use a tapered offcut to direct clamping pressure square across the joint.

Glue and screw aprons to legs. McBrien arrays the screws in an X pattern at each joint. To avoid adding twist to the assembly, he makes sure the parts are flush to the foam when he drives the screws. Be sure to make the cutout for the vise before this step.

Bracing comes next. These short pieces also are glued and screwed in place. To keep parts square so the top lies flat, McBrien aligns the face of each brace with a square when driving the screws.

You'll need to cut out part of the front apron to accommodate the vise's threads and travel rods. Make the cutout as small as possible to minimize weakening the apron. Also, if the vise ends up more than 6 in. or so from a side apron or bracing, add another strip of bracing next to it for more support. To bolt the vise in place, you'll need to add blocking to the MDF top and the apron. It should be robust enough to accept coarse-threaded lag bolts, although the exact size you'll need will depend on your specific vise. To protect your work from the vise's metal jaws, screw some thick hardwood to the jaw's faces.

To mimic an end vise, I drill a row of dog holes along the front of the benchtop and pair them with a Veritas Wonder Pup. It has a post that fits into the holes and an adjustable head that screws in and out, letting you clamp a workpiece against a benchdog. I like brass dogs, also from Veritas. The duo works great for edge-planing.

SHELF

Ledge helps hold stretchers in place. To hold the stretchers at the right height, McBrien screws an offcut to each leg assembly. This frees up his hands for attaching the stretchers (top). The block can stay or be removed. Bracing (above) will support the shelf. Hold these boards tightly to prevent them from twisting.

Two-piece shelf. It's impossible to slip in a full-size shelf, so use two long, narrow boards instead. Screw these to the stretchers and bracing.

TOP

Tip the base onto the top. McBrien lines up the base so there's an even 3-in. overhang from the aprons.

Glue blocks secure top to base. MDF is poor at holding screws, so McBrien uses glue blocks to secure the base to the top. These blocks are glued and screwed to the MDF but simply screwed to the aprons and bracing in case the top ever needs to be replaced.

Vise

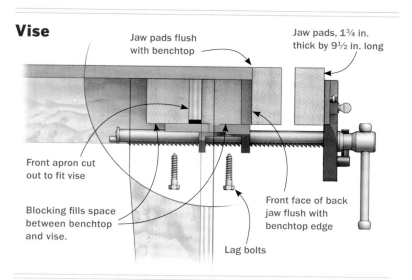

Jaw pads flush with benchtop

Jaw pads, 1¾ in. thick by 9½ in. long

Front apron cut out to fit vise

Blocking fills space between benchtop and vise.

Front face of back jaw flush with benchtop edge

Lag bolts

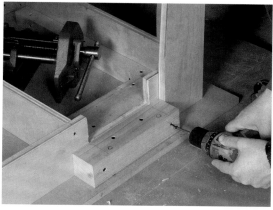

Vise needs blocking. These blocks give you a place to drive the bolts for attaching the vise. They also bolster the front apron, which will be under a lot of stress from the vise.

Hardwood jaw pads protect work. Rip these wide enough so they extend just above the top of the bench. McBrien uses maple here, but any hardwood will do.

Lag bolts and washers secure vise to bench. These need to be thick, coarse bolts to hold the heavy vise in place. Predrill large enough holes for them to avoid splitting the blocking.

Plane down the jaw pads. You want the pads to be flush with the benchtop.

Good Dogs

McBrien drills a series of dog holes at the front of the bench and a single hole at the back in line with his vise to use with a stop. Feel free to drill a hole wherever you feel is necessary, though.

REAR HOLE PAIRS DOG WITH PLANING STOP

FRONT HOLES PAIR DOG WITH VERITAS WONDER PUP

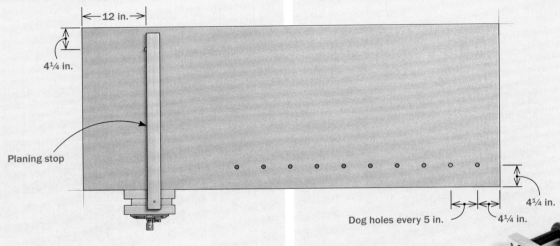

← 12 in. →

4¼ in.

Planing stop

Dog holes every 5 in.

4¼ in.

4¼ in.

The planing stop is simply a wide, thin board screwed to a cleat that gets clamped in the vise. Its far end is supported by a benchdog.

This setup mimics an end vise. The Wonder Pup is an adjustable bar that pinches stock against a benchdog, letting you edge-plane long stock on the bench—which is more secure than doing it in the front vise.

Build a Stout Workbench

CHRIS GOCHNOUR

I've done a fair amount of handplaning during my 32 years as a professional furniture maker, and I've found that the best way to secure a board for face-planing is between two benchdogs, which can be set below the board's surface so you can plane without hindrance. Clamps and holdfasts, by contrast, seem always to be in the way. And unlike a planing stop, dogs have no trouble holding the board in place when you plane diagonally or across the grain.

Heavy-Duty Workbench

With a strong base and a well-designed top, this bench is a streamlined workhorse. Equip it with a tail vise, and you're ready for just about anything.

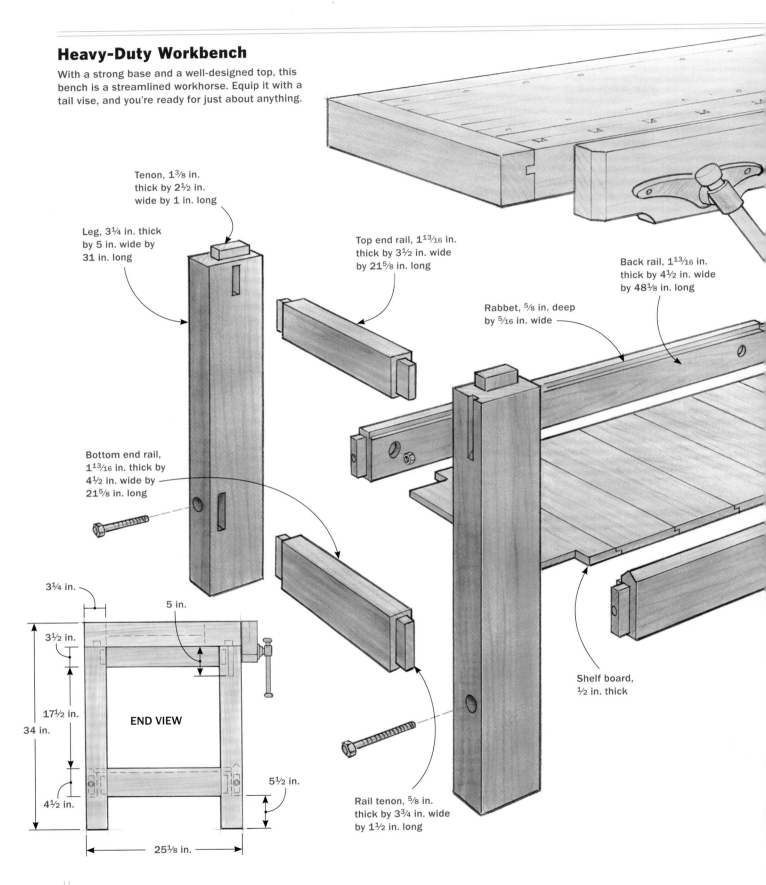

Tenon, $1^3/8$ in. thick by $2^1/2$ in. wide by 1 in. long

Leg, $3^1/4$ in. thick by 5 in. wide by 31 in. long

Top end rail, $1^{13}/16$ in. thick by $3^1/2$ in. wide by $21^5/8$ in. long

Back rail, $1^{13}/16$ in. thick by $4^1/2$ in. wide by $48^1/8$ in. long

Rabbet, $5/8$ in. deep by $5/16$ in. wide

Bottom end rail, $1^{13}/16$ in. thick by $4^1/2$ in. wide by $21^5/8$ in. long

Shelf board, $1/2$ in. thick

Rail tenon, $5/8$ in. thick by $3^3/4$ in. wide by $1^1/2$ in. long

$3^1/4$ in.

5 in.

$3^1/2$ in.

$17^1/2$ in.

34 in.

END VIEW

$4^1/2$ in.

$5^1/2$ in.

$25^1/8$ in.

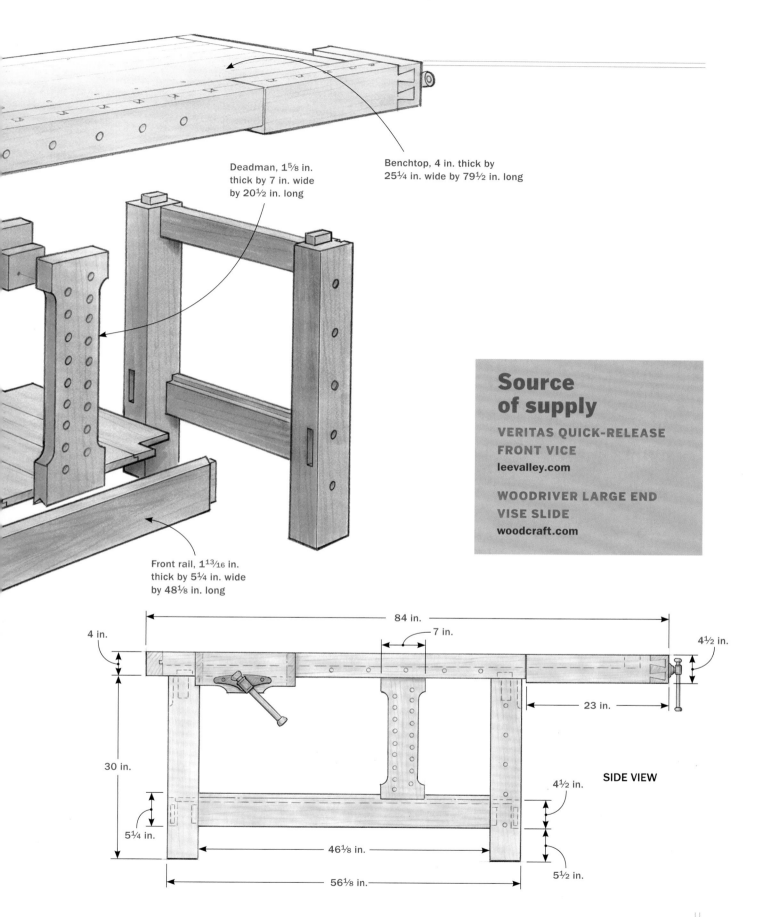

Deadman, 1⅝ in. thick by 7 in. wide by 20½ in. long

Benchtop, 4 in. thick by 25¼ in. wide by 79½ in. long

Front rail, 1¹³⁄₁₆ in. thick by 5¼ in. wide by 48⅛ in. long

Source of supply

VERITAS QUICK-RELEASE FRONT VICE
leevalley.com

WOODRIVER LARGE END VISE SLIDE
woodcraft.com

84 in.

7 in.

4 in.

4½ in.

23 in.

30 in.

5¼ in.

4½ in.

46⅛ in.

5½ in.

56⅛ in.

SIDE VIEW

Versatile and effective. A traditional tail vise excels at everything from face- and edge-planing to cutting tenons, a range that other end vises can't match.

Benchdogs require a vise, and when I build a workbench, I like to locate that vise on the end. There are four options for an end vise: a traditional tail vise, a wagon vise, a metal face vise mounted on the end, and a twin-screw vise. All four can be used for face-planing boards, but the tail vise has several advantages over the others. With a tail vise, the dog holes can be placed very close to the bench's front edge, which makes it possible to plane narrow boards with a plough plane or similar plane that has a fence that hangs below the

Build a Better Benchtop

A top needs to be heavy and inflexible, but you can get that by combining a moderately thick center section with two beefy edges.

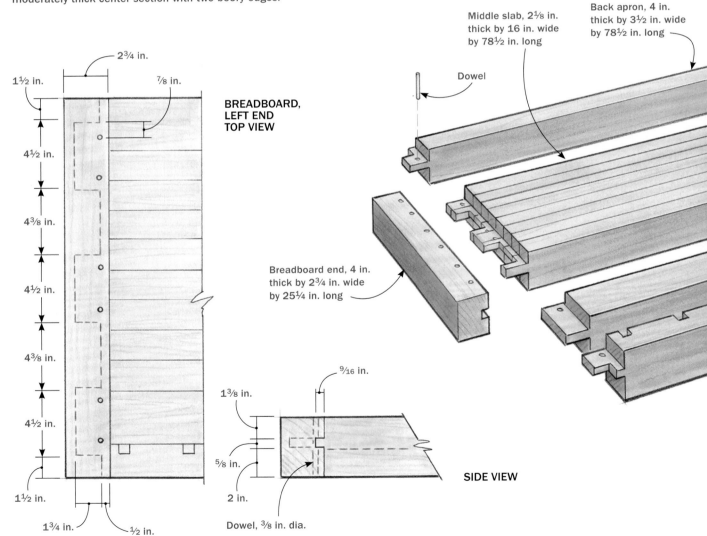

2¾ in.

1½ in. 7⁄8 in.

BREADBOARD, LEFT END TOP VIEW

4½ in.

4⅜ in.

4½ in.

4⅜ in.

4½ in.

1½ in.

1¾ in. ½ in.

Middle slab, 2⅛ in. thick by 16 in. wide by 78½ in. long

Back apron, 4 in. thick by 3½ in. wide by 78½ in. long

Dowel

Breadboard end, 4 in. thick by 2¾ in. wide by 25¼ in. long

9⁄16 in.

1⅜ in.

5⁄8 in.

2 in.

Dowel, ⅜ in. dia.

SIDE VIEW

benchtop. That's something that isn't possible with a steel vise. Wagon vises work great when the board is flat on the benchtop, but with a tail vise you can also clamp a workpiece vertically, which lets you cut tenons, for example. The fourth option, the twin-screw vise, handles tenons and edge-planing fine, but it doesn't support work as well as a tail vise for face-planing. These advantages are why I chose a tail vise for my bench.

For many woodworkers, building and installing a tail vise seems intimidating, but it shouldn't be. I've installed quite a few, both on benches of my own and on student benches, and have developed a process that ensures the vise slides smoothly and doesn't snag. I'll show you how I do it.

The top is thick where it needs to be

Making a bench is a big undertaking, but fortunately most of the work involved is fairly routine. The base of this bench is four big legs joined to the rails between them with

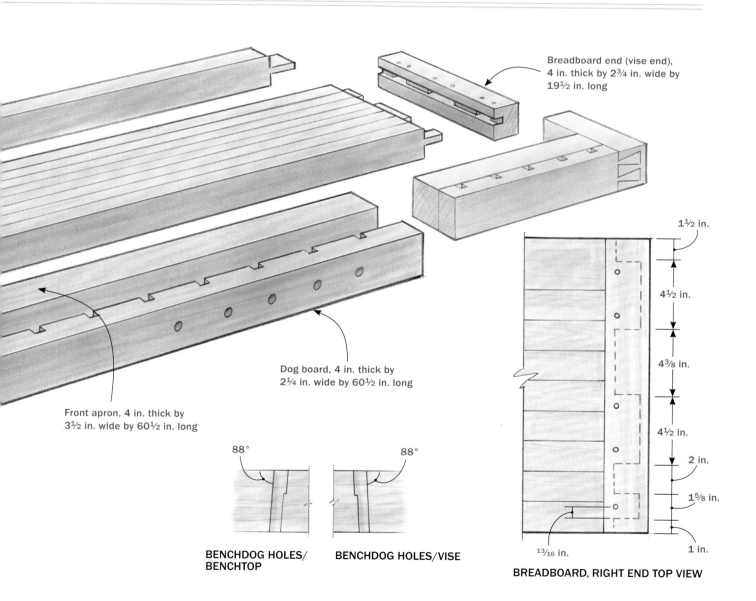

Breadboard end (vise end), 4 in. thick by 2¾ in. wide by 19½ in. long

Dog board, 4 in. thick by 2¼ in. wide by 60½ in. long

Front apron, 4 in. thick by 3½ in. wide by 60½ in. long

88°

88°

BENCHDOG HOLES/ BENCHTOP

BENCHDOG HOLES/VISE

1½ in.

4½ in.

4⅜ in.

4½ in.

2 in.

1⅝ in.

1 in.

¹³⁄₁₆ in.

BREADBOARD, RIGHT END TOP VIEW

Cut angled dadoes for the benchdog holes. Use a dado head and a miter gauge to remove most of the waste from the dog holes.

Rout the final shape. A template ensures that all of the dog holes are identical. Because the dog holes in the vise jaw face the opposite direction from those in the benchtop, Gochnour uses a template that has a pattern for both directions (top). The pattern has a notch so that a flush-trimming bit creates the pocket into which the dog's head fits (above).

mortise-and-tenon joints. Shiplapped boards set between the lower rails provide a nice place for storing jigs and anything else you like to keep close by. I am going to skip over the base construction here, because the process is relatively straightforward, and focus instead on the top and the tail vise.

The benchtop is thick along the front and back edges but has a wide, thinner section between. The middle doesn't need to be as thick, because all the pounding on a bench should be done over a leg or a top rail. This bench has a thick back apron and a front section made up of a thick front apron and an equally thick dog board. Glue up the thinner middle section, and then mill the back apron, front apron, and dog board to their final dimensions.

Next cut the dog holes in the dog board. The dogs should angle inward. To make that happen, the dog holes in the benchtop slant 2° toward the vise; in the vise, they lean toward the benchtop. I make the dog holes in two steps. First I hog out the waste with a

dado set at the tablesaw. Then I use a router and template to refine the hole and add a wider section at the top so that a dog, which has a head that's wider than its shaft, can fit completely into the hole. Cut the dog holes in the vise jaw at this time, too.

After you've completed the dog holes, glue the dog board to the front apron. Let the glue dry, and then glue the three parts of the top together. Give the glue a night to dry before installing the breadboard ends. You're done with the top for now. It's time to get busy making the tail vise.

Glue the dog board to the front apron.
Spread glue only on the dog board, and keep the glue about ½ in. from the dog holes (above left). Gochnour uses Festool Dominoes for alignment and plenty of clamps, alternating them from top to bottom (left).

Bring it all together.
A plywood spacer under the center section keeps it aligned with the thicker front and back sections. Be sure to add clamps above the top to prevent the thicker sections from slanting inward on the bottom.

Build the Core of the Tail Vise

The success of a tail vise depends on how well the wooden jaw and metal hardware work together. Start with the vise's hollow core, which is the key to smooth operation.

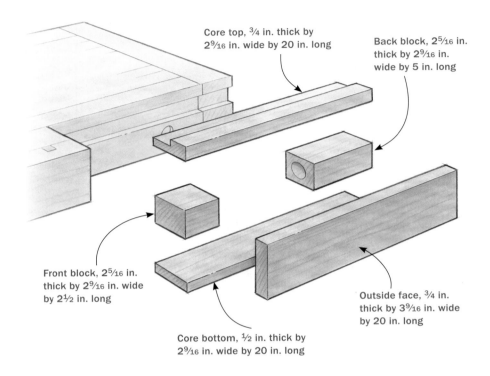

Core top, ¾ in. thick by 2⁹⁄₁₆ in. wide by 20 in. long

Back block, 2⁵⁄₁₆ in. thick by 2⁹⁄₁₆ in. wide by 5 in. long

Front block, 2⁵⁄₁₆ in. thick by 2⁹⁄₁₆ in. wide by 2½ in. long

Core bottom, ½ in. thick by 2⁹⁄₁₆ in. wide by 20 in. long

Outside face, ¾ in. thick by 3⁹⁄₁₆ in. wide by 20 in. long

Make the tail vise in stages

At the heart of this tail vise is some metal hardware. A vertical plate that holds the nut face-mounts to the benchtop. A pair of slides screwed to the wooden jaw grasp the plate. The screw goes through the jaw and threads into the top slide. The jaw has three parts: a hollow core, the vise dog board, and the end cap. Because the vise's success rides on how well you join the hardware to the core, it's best to start there. Get it right, and then add the dog board and end cap.

The core begins by gluing together four parts: a top and bottom, and a front and back block. A large space in the middle accommodates the vise screw and nut. After the glue has dried, add the outside face to the core. What you have now is akin to a box without a lid. Take it to the drill press and drill a clearance hole through the back end for the vise screw. Next, cut a rabbet in the core top. The vise's top slide fits into this rabbet. Clamp the two slides, with the mounting plate between them, to the core, and mark the holes where the bolts go through the bottom slide and thread into the top slide. Unclamp the slides and drill clearance holes for the bolts.

Cap the core. After gluing the four pieces of the vise core together, glue it to the outside face, using a piece of melamine to keep them aligned.

Cut a rabbet in the core top. The easiest way to make this wide rabbet is with two cuts at the tablesaw. The vise's top slide fits into the rabbet.

Make way for the vise screw. It takes some serious clamping and an extender for the Forstner bit, but it is possible to drill the hole at the drill press. A fence on the drill-press table helps keep the vise core plumb.

Slides are attached with bolts. Clamp the slides to the core with the vise plate between them. Transfer the bolt hole locations from both slides and then drill the holes at the drill press, coming halfway in from both sides.

Fit the Core to the Bench

Attach the hardware to the bench, and get the vise core riding smoothly on it before you go any further with the vise construction.

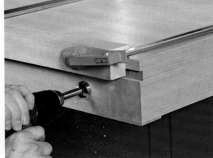

Groove the top. Two passes with a rabbeting bit create a slot into which the top slide fits.

Mortise for the nut. The vise screw's nut has a threaded stud that passes through the vise plate. A nut that secures it from behind the plate fits into a shallow mortise. Clamp a straightedge to the benchtop and register the vise plate against it. Transfer the hole to the bench (left). Drill the mortise with a Forstner bit (right).

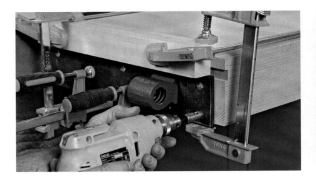

Screw on the vise plate. Use a Vix bit to center a pilot hole for each screw, and then drive the screws. Make sure the screw heads sit below the surface of the vise plate.

Assemble in place. Gochnour bolts on the slides while clamps hold the vise core snug against the vise plate. Threaded up from the bottom, the bolts are still accessible after the vise is complete.

Check the glide. Now's the time to test how well the vise slides. You can trim the rabbet if it's too loose or add a shim under the bottom slide if it's too tight.

Now mount the plate to the benchtop and install the vise core on the plate, as shown in the sidebar on the facing page. Give it a slide. If it's too loose, take a shaving or two from the rabbet and try again. If it's too tight, shim the bottom slide. When the core glides smoothly, move on to the dog board and end cap.

The dog board gets a few dovetails; the end cap gets the pins. After you've cut and fitted the joint, but before you glue the two parts together, drill a hole through the end cap for the vise screw. Then cut slots for the slip tenons that join the end cap to the core and top plate. Glue the jaw and end cap together and then glue that assembly to the vise core.

Finish the Tail Vise

With the hollow core complete, add the dog board, top plate, and end cap to finish the jaw.

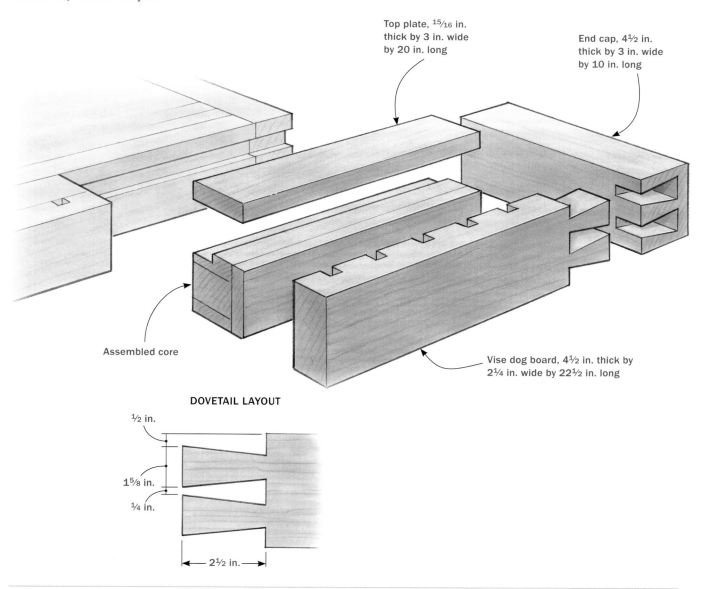

Top plate, 15/16 in. thick by 3 in. wide by 20 in. long

End cap, 4½ in. thick by 3 in. wide by 10 in. long

Assembled core

Vise dog board, 4½ in. thick by 2¼ in. wide by 22½ in. long

DOVETAIL LAYOUT

½ in.

1⅝ in.

¼ in.

2½ in.

Dovetail the corner. This is the traditional way to join the end cap and dog board. It's strong and looks great.

Add the core. Keep the glue away from the dog holes (left). When clamping, use a caul to bridge the hole in the vise core (right).

Glue on the top plate. It should sit about 1/16 in. above the benchtop. Gochnour uses a Festool Domino to strengthen its connection to the end cap (above). Apply clamping pressure both side to side and along the plate's length (right). Then add clamps for top to bottom pressure.

The last step in making the vise is to glue on the top plate.

You're ready to mount the completed vise. Check how the jaw closes against the bench. Use a bevel-up plane to shave the jaw's end grain until the vise closes nice and tight. Finally, plane the tail vise flush to the benchtop. Now you can get to work.

Install the vise. Hook the top slide over the vise plate, put the bottom slide in place, and then bolt them together.

Make it flush. After refining the end of the jaw so that it closes tightly against the bench, plane down the tail vise level with the benchtop.

Shaker Workbench

MICHAEL PEKOVICH
AND MATT KENNEY

The shop at *Fine Woodworking* gets a lot of use and a fair amount of abuse. This is especially true of the workbench. After years of steady and heavy use, the top and vises are just hanging on, and the tool cabinet in the base is barely functional. The time for a new bench has come.

You might think that a bench for a communal shop would need to be quite different from a bench used in a one-man shop. But the basic requirements are the same. It should have a thick, flat top that sits on a stout, rigid base, and it should offer plenty of options for holding work. The bench we designed has it all. Inspired by the one used in the workshop at Hancock Shaker Village in Pittsfield, Mass., the bench has a big, heavy base with drawers for all of your hand tools, and a beefy hard-maple top.

For holding work, we put a twin-screw vise on the front, with enough space between the screws to dovetail most furniture parts. We added a sliding board jack to support boards for edge planing, or for when you need to dovetail a part that's too big to fit in the vise. For planing work on the benchtop, we prefer using stops tailored for the job at hand. That's why there is no end vise. The top can also be drilled for holdfasts.

In general, benches are not complicated beasts. The most challenging part of building this one is handling the big parts as you cut joinery in them. By the way, even though two of us built the bench together, it's certainly possible for just one woodworker to get the job done.

Begin with the base

There are two parts to the base: a stout frame and a cabinet with drawers. Construction begins with the frame, which is made of 8/4 cherry. The mortise-and-tenon joints connecting the legs to the rails and stretchers are drawbored, eliminating the need to clamp the base together as the glue dries. The back and sides of the frame are grooved to accept shiplapped panels, which are made of white pine and finished with blue milk paint.

After gluing up the blanks for the legs and the three stretchers, mill all of the frame parts to their final dimensions, then lay out the mortises, including the holes for the drawbore pegs. Drill those holes at the drill press before mortising.

We cut the mortises with a hollow-chisel mortiser. We used a ½-in. bit to cut the ½-in.-wide mortises in the short side rails. However, for the 1-in.-wide mortises in the stretchers, we used a ⅜-in. bit and cut them in two passes. Cut one side of the mortise, flip the board around (the mortise is centered on the leg), and cut the other side. To remove the ¼-in. bridge of waste in the middle, just plunge the bit into the waste, working from one end to the other.

Before moving on to the tenons, cut notches in the top of the front legs for the

Proven design, modern hardware

With a thick top, a beefy enclosed base, and drawers for your tools, this bench has Shaker bones. The twin-screw vise is a smart, modern update.

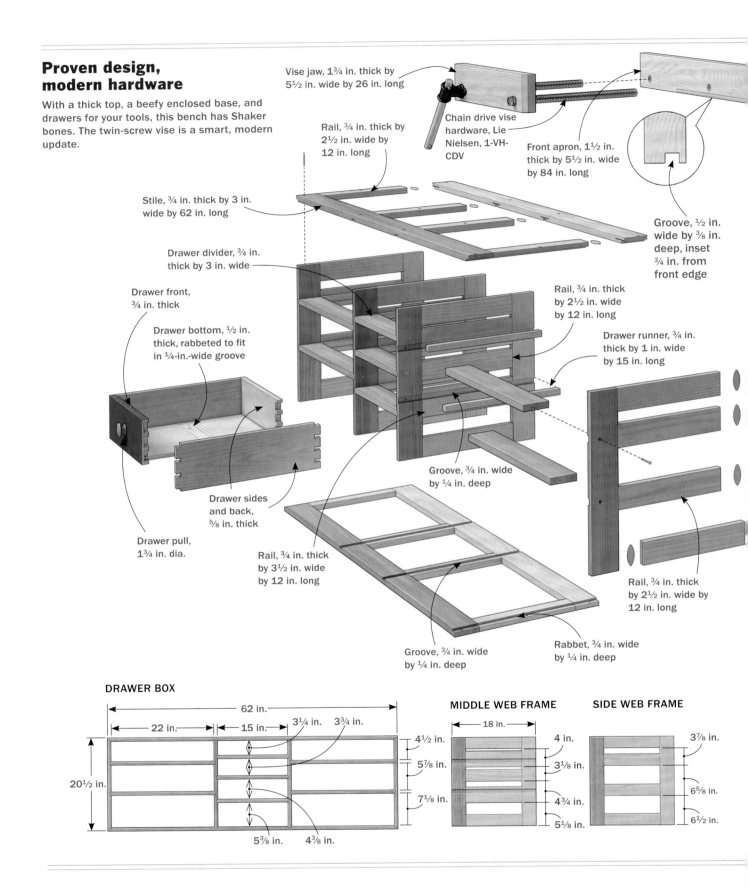

Vise jaw, 1¾ in. thick by 5½ in. wide by 26 in. long

Chain drive vise hardware, Lie Nielsen, 1-VH-CDV

Front apron, 1½ in. thick by 5½ in. wide by 84 in. long

Rail, ¾ in. thick by 2½ in. wide by 12 in. long

Groove, ½ in. wide by ⅜ in. deep, inset ¾ in. from front edge

Stile, ¾ in. thick by 3 in. wide by 62 in. long

Drawer divider, ¾ in. thick by 3 in. wide

Rail, ¾ in. thick by 2½ in. wide by 12 in. long

Drawer front, ¾ in. thick

Drawer bottom, ½ in. thick, rabbeted to fit in ¼-in.-wide groove

Drawer runner, ¾ in. thick by 1 in. wide by 15 in. long

Drawer sides and back, ⅝ in. thick

Groove, ¾ in. wide by ¼ in. deep

Drawer pull, 1¾ in. dia.

Rail, ¾ in. thick by 3½ in. wide by 12 in. long

Rail, ¾ in. thick by 2½ in. wide by 12 in. long

Groove, ¾ in. wide by ¼ in. deep

Rabbet, ¾ in. wide by ¼ in. deep

DRAWER BOX

62 in.

22 in.

15 in.

3¼ in.

3¾ in.

4½ in.

5⅞ in.

7⅛ in.

20½ in.

5⅜ in.

4⅜ in.

MIDDLE WEB FRAME

18 in.

4 in.

3⅛ in.

4¾ in.

5⅛ in.

SIDE WEB FRAME

3⅞ in.

6⅝ in.

6½ in.

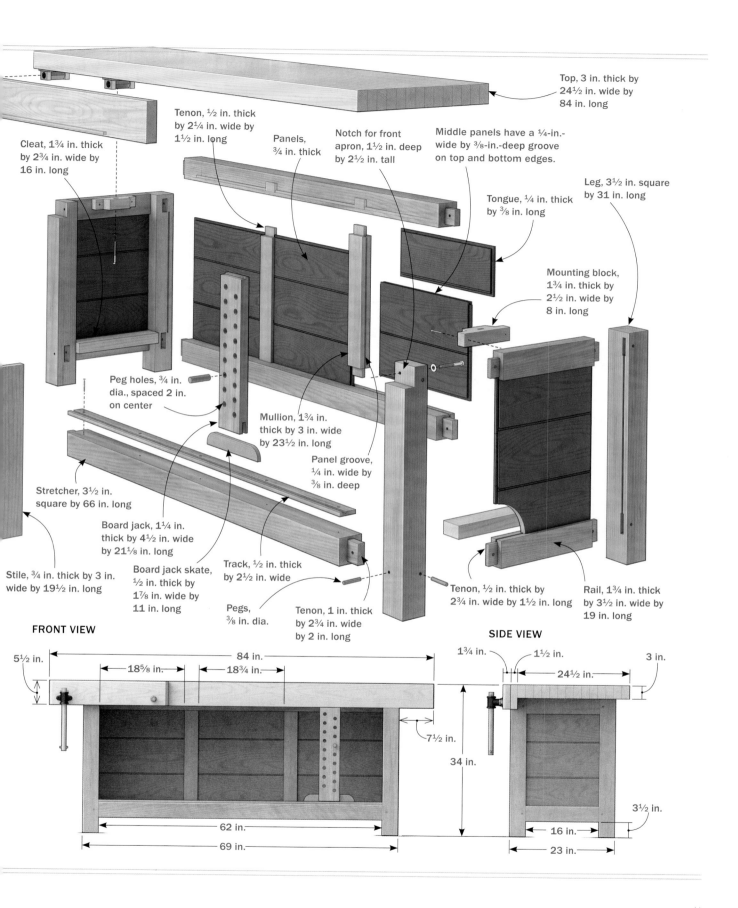

Top, 3 in. thick by 24½ in. wide by 84 in. long

Cleat, 1¾ in. thick by 2¾ in. wide by 16 in. long

Tenon, ½ in. thick by 2¼ in. wide by 1½ in. long

Panels, ¾ in. thick

Notch for front apron, 1½ in. deep by 2½ in. tall

Middle panels have a ¼-in.-wide by ⅜-in.-deep groove on top and bottom edges.

Tongue, ¼ in. thick by ⅜ in. long

Leg, 3½ in. square by 31 in. long

Mounting block, 1¾ in. thick by 2½ in. wide by 8 in. long

Peg holes, ¾ in. dia., spaced 2 in. on center

Mullion, 1¾ in. thick by 3 in. wide by 23½ in. long

Panel groove, ¼ in. wide by ⅜ in. deep

Stretcher, 3½ in. square by 66 in. long

Board jack, 1¼ in. thick by 4½ in. wide by 21⅛ in. long

Stile, ¾ in. thick by 3 in. wide by 19½ in. long

Board jack skate, ½ in. thick by 1⅞ in. wide by 11 in. long

Track, ½ in. thick by 2½ in. wide

Pegs, ⅜ in. dia.

Tenon, 1 in. thick by 2¾ in. wide by 2 in. long

Tenon, ½ in. thick by 2¾ in. wide by 1½ in. long

Rail, 1¾ in. thick by 3½ in. wide by 19 in. long

FRONT VIEW

5½ in.

84 in.

18⅝ in.

18¾ in.

7½ in.

62 in.

69 in.

SIDE VIEW

1¾ in.

1½ in.

3 in.

24½ in.

34 in.

3½ in.

16 in.

23 in.

Mortise-and-tenons come first. When cutting the large mortises, size the bit to leave a thin bridge between the two outside cuts. Easily removed later, this bridge supports the bit and keeps it from deflecting during the second cut.

apron. These notches allow the apron to be flush with the front of the legs, giving you more bearing surface when clamping in the vise. (Don't worry about the apron interfering with the top front stretcher—there is none.) We cut the shoulder of the notch at the tablesaw, and the cheek at the bandsaw, cleaning up the surfaces with a handplane. Drill a clearance hole in the notch for the lag screw that you will use later to secure the apron to the base.

Cut the tenons on the rails of the end assemblies at the tablesaw, using a miter gauge and dado set. The stretchers are too long for the tenons to be cut the same way. For these, the best approach is to cut the shoulders at the tablesaw and the cheeks at the bandsaw. Leave the tenon just a bit thick, and trim it to fit.

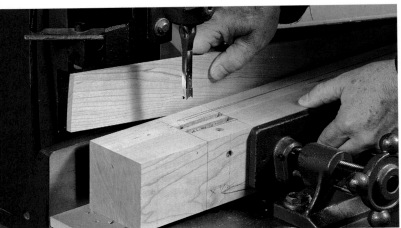

Outside walls first. After cutting along the first wall, rotate the leg so that the opposite face is against the fence, then cut along the second edge (top). To remove the waste between cuts, insert a spacer between the fence and the workpiece (middle above), and remove the bridge in the center (above).

Two tools for stretcher tenons. Cut the shoulders at the tablesaw first. On the bandsaw, set the fence for the first cheek, cut it, then flip the stretcher to cut the second cheek.

Cut grooves for back and side panels. The frame of the base forms a nearly indestructible foundation for woodworking, and it also holds the panels that turn the base into a cabinet. The through-grooves are straightforward. Add an auxiliary face to the rip fence. Rip the groove in line with the tenon.

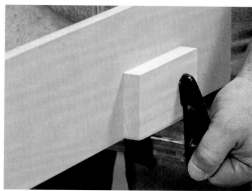

Stopped grooves need stop blocks. Clamp a block to the auxiliary fence (above). Place the trailing end of the leg against the stop, then carefully lower the leg onto the spinning dado set (right). Screwed to the outfeed table, a piece of MDF terminates the cut (below right). Turn off the saw before removing the leg.

Next, mark the tenons for drawboring. To learn how this is done, take a look at Steve Latta's article "Drawbore Your Tenons," *Fine Woodworking* #241, p. 38.

With the mortise-and-tenon joinery complete, turn to the grooves for the panels. On the stretchers and rails, these are through-grooves, but on the legs they are stopped. Still, you can cut them all at the tablesaw with a dado set. The through-grooves are no problem, but use stop blocks to help start

Two coats of paint. Because it's mixed with water, milk paint raises the grain, so sand with 320-grit paper after each coat.

Bead the top and bottom panels. On the top panel, the bottom edge gets the bead. On the bottom panel, the top edge gets beaded.

Assemble the base. This is a big base, but you don't need long clamps to assemble it because the drawbore pegs will lock the joints tight. Start with the ends first. Add the rails to one of the legs, then slide the panels in place. The second leg completes the assembly.

and stop the cut for the stopped grooves (see photos, p. 57).

For the tongue-and-groove panels, begin by cutting the boards to their final dimensions. Cut all of the ¼-in.-wide grooves with a dado set, then cut the tongues. The tongues are centered on the boards, and the same dado and fence setup is used to cut the tongues that fit into the grooves in the base frame. To cut the small bead on the groove side of the joints, we used a router bit. Paint all the panels before assembly. Two coats should do the job (sand between coats with 320-grit paper).

The last thing to do before assembling the base is to make the pegs. We used white oak

Drawbore the joints. Use straightgrained white oak for the pegs. The drawboring action eliminates the need for clamps. The pegs are trimmed flush later.

and made the pegs with a dowel plate. If you don't have a dowel plate, just buy white oak dowel stock at a woodworking-supply store, and cut it to length.

With pegs made, you're ready to assemble the base. Begin with the ends. Glue two rails into one leg, then slide the panels into the grooves (no glue). Spread glue on the two remaining joints and add the second leg. Finally, drive in the drawbore pegs for all four joints.

After the two end assemblies are together, glue and drawbore the three stretchers to one of the end assemblies. Slide the back panels in place. Finally, glue and drawbore the stretchers to the other end assembly.

Glue up the top and add the vise

The next job is the top. It's not hard to make, but it does require some serious muscle. The best way to tackle the top is to glue it up in sections that are narrow enough to run across your jointer and through the planer after the glue has dried. After you have milled the sections to their final thickness, glue them together.

While the top dries, cut the apron to size. Then use the drill press to drill holes in it for the vise. Next, rout the groove for the sliding board jack on the bottom edge of the apron using a spiral upcut bit. To prevent the router from wandering, we attached two edge guides to it, one on each side of the apron. With that done, glue the apron to the top and install the vise.

There are two more things to do before you put the top on the base. Glue the mounting blocks to the top rails of the end assemblies. These are drilled with a clearance hole and counterbore for the lag screws that attach the top. Also, attach the drawer-box cleats.

Some help required. After putting the front stretcher and assembled back into one of the ends, lower the second end into place. It's heavy, so ask a friend for help.

Attach the apron with the top in place. Resting the apron on the notches in the legs keeps it level, and makes it easier to get the first few clamps on. You'll need a lot of clamps. Plane it flush after the glue dries.

Build and install the drawer box. Because the base is enclosed, there is no need to make a heavy solid wood or plywood cabinet for the drawers. A skeletal box made from six frames held together by biscuits and screws is all you need. The frame is screwed to, and reinforced by, the bench's base. After cutting the grooves for the drawer runners in the vertical frames, screw them to the horizontal frames.

Add the dividers. These slide in from the front (left), and are held in place by screws driven through the vertical dividers. Then glue the runners in place (right). They also serve as kickers for the drawers beneath them.

Slide the box in. Screw it to the lower stretchers and cleats attached to the lower rails.

Build the drawer cabinet

We could have built the structure for the drawers into the base, but that approach is unnecessarily complicated. Instead, we built a frame "box" to create the drawer pockets and then slid that into the base.

The frame is constructed from two horizontal and four vertical web frames. The two middle frames fit into dadoes cut into the horizontal dividers. The two end frames fit into rabbets.

This drawer box will not shoulder any significant weight, so you don't need mortise-and-tenon joints to hold it together. We used biscuits and screws. After the frames have been assembled, cut the grooves and rabbets in the top and bottom frames to accept the vertical frames. Use the same dado setup to cut the drawer-runner grooves in the vertical frames.

Assemble the drawer box with screws and then slide it into the bench base. Screw the bottom frame to the lower stretchers.

Now make and install the dividers and runners/kickers. The dividers are screwed

Board jack is a helping hand. Panels too wide to fit between the screws of the vise, or boards so long that they are more outside than inside the jaws, need extra support to keep them steady. This board jack is the perfect assistant. The board jack rides in a track. After cutting the groove in the track, screw it to the bottom stretcher.

into the frame, but the runners/kickers are glued in place.

With the drawer box complete, you can make and install the drawers. After that, it's time for the board jack. The bottom edge of the apron is already grooved for it. Make and install the grooved track that sits on the bottom stretcher. The jack has two parts. There's a vertical piece with two rows of holes. It's rabbeted on top to fit into the apron's groove and notched on the bottom to take the second part of the jack: a skate that fits into the track.

You're almost done. Use a straightedge and winding sticks to check if the top is flat. If it's not, plane it flat. Finally, apply a penetrating oil finish to the bench, including the milk-painted surfaces. After the oil dries, get to work on your next piece of furniture, and have some fun.

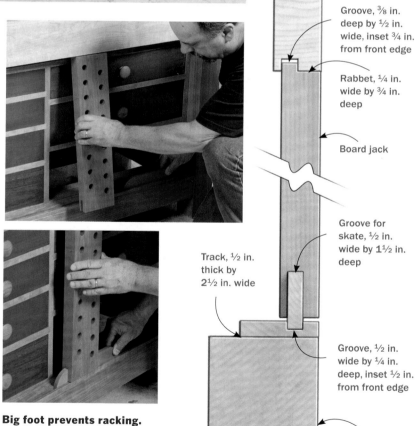

Big foot prevents racking. The long skate at the bottom of the jack allows it to slide more smoothly. Attach it with screws.

Front apron

Groove, ⅜ in. deep by ½ in. wide, inset ¾ in. from front edge

Rabbet, ¼ in. wide by ¾ in. deep

Board jack

Groove for skate, ½ in. wide by 1½ in. deep

Track, ½ in. thick by 2½ in. wide

Groove, ½ in. wide by ¼ in. deep, inset ½ in. from front edge

Bottom stretcher

Modified Roubo Is the Ultimate Workbench

JEFF MILLER

Most woodworkers build only one workbench. I've had the luxury of building seven so far. Why so many? Partly because I need extra benches in my shop for teaching classes. But also because I love having benches that excel at holding different kinds of work.

With all the different benches and vises in my shop, I thought I'd experienced

Leg Vise

Wagon Vise

WAGON VISE

Strong vise, solid benchtop. Based on a traditional design, the Benchcrafted wagon vise provides benchdog clamping without a large movable jaw to compromise the integrity of the top. The vise can also be used to clamp boards vertically (right).

about everything in the realm of workbenches. But a year ago I built a small bench to test out two new vises from Benchcrafted that had caught my eye—one a leg vise and the other a wagon vise (see Tools & Materials, *Fine Woodworking* #225). Both are based on traditional designs but updated with wheel-style handles and acme threads, and built to exceptional standards of quality. For all-around work-holding, these vises were a revelation. They held more securely and were easier to adjust than any other vises I've used.

LEG VISE

A leg vise with leverage. Another take on an old design, Benchcrafted's leg vise is versatile, powerful, and silky smooth in use. To keep the jaw parallel to a workpiece, you place a pin in one of a series of holes in the parallel guide (left).

Spin the wheel with one finger and the vises closed on a workpiece with a convincing thonk. They were also easier to install than many other vises. Before I'd had the use of the new bench for a month, it had become my favorite, and I decided that I needed to make a full-size version using Benchcrafted vise hardware.

Powerhouse vises left and right

The bench I built is a modified Roubo-style with a very heavy top and a beefy base. What makes it a Roubo (André Jacob Roubo was a French cabinetmaker in the 1700s who wrote an influential treatise on woodworking) is the massive size, the blocky legs flush to the front edge of the benchtop, and the leg vise, a centuries-old style with a huge jaw that offers superb clamping pressure and lots of space for the workpiece. To function properly, a leg vise requires that the front edge of the benchtop be in the same plane with the front face of the leg.

The vise screw is 8 in. below the surface of the bench, allowing the vise to accommodate

Bombproof bench

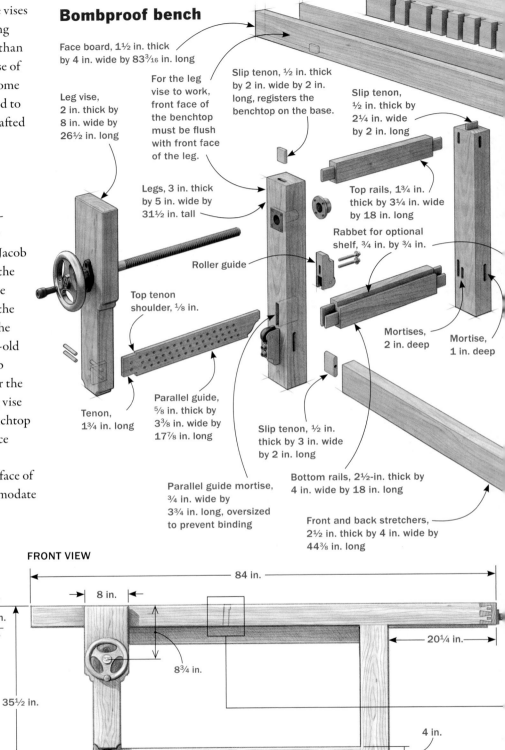

Face board, 1½ in. thick by 4 in. wide by 83³⁄₁₆ in. long

For the leg vise to work, front face of the benchtop must be flush with front face of the leg.

Slip tenon, ½ in. thick by 2 in. wide by 2 in. long, registers the benchtop on the base.

Slip tenon, ½ in. thick by 2¼ in. wide by 2 in. long

Leg vise, 2 in. thick by 8 in. wide by 26½ in. long

Legs, 3 in. thick by 5 in. wide by 31½ in. tall

Top rails, 1¾ in. thick by 3¼ in. wide by 18 in. long

Rabbet for optional shelf, ¾ in. by ¾ in.

Roller guide

Top tenon shoulder, ⅛ in.

Mortises, 2 in. deep

Mortise, 1 in. deep

Tenon, 1¾ in. long

Parallel guide, ⅝ in. thick by 3⅜ in. wide by 17⅞ in. long

Slip tenon, ½ in. thick by 3 in. wide by 2 in. long

Parallel guide mortise, ¾ in. wide by 3¾ in. long, oversized to prevent binding

Bottom rails, 2½-in. thick by 4 in. wide by 18 in. long

Front and back stretchers, 2½ in. thick by 4 in. wide by 44⅜ in. long

END VIEW

2 in.
24¼ in.
3³¹⁄₃₂ in.
5 in.
12 in.
4 in.
35½ in.
24 in.

FRONT VIEW

84 in.
8 in.
8¾ in.
20¼ in.
4 in.
5 in.
54⅜ in.

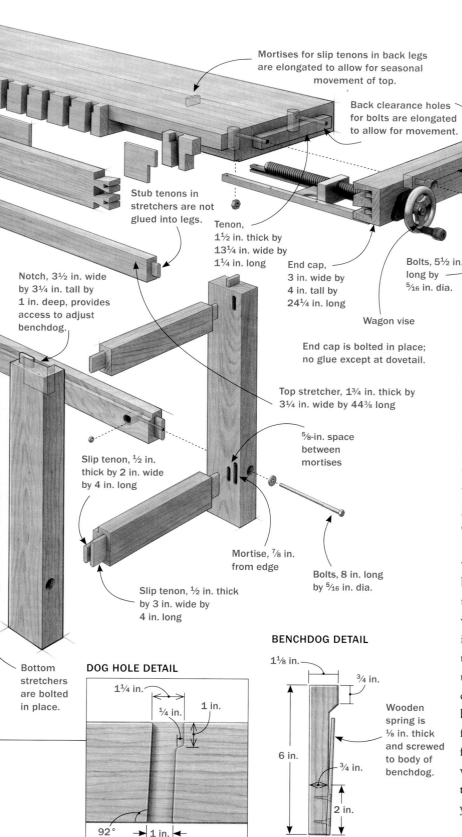

Mortises for slip tenons in back legs are elongated to allow for seasonal movement of top.

Back clearance holes for bolts are elongated to allow for movement.

Stub tenons in stretchers are not glued into legs.

Tenon, 1½ in. thick by 13¼ in. wide by 1¼ in. long

Notch, 3½ in. wide by 3¼ in. tall by 1 in. deep, provides access to adjust benchdog.

End cap, 3 in. wide by 4 in. tall by 24¼ in. long

Wagon vise

End cap is bolted in place; no glue except at dovetail.

Bolts, 5½ in. long by 5⁄16 in. dia.

Mortise, 13¾ in. wide

Top stretcher, 1¾ in. thick by 3¼ in. wide by 44⅜ long

5⁄8-in. space between mortises

Slip tenon, ½ in. thick by 2 in. wide by 4 in. long

Mortise, 7⁄8 in. from edge

Bolts, 8 in. long by 5⁄16 in. dia.

Slip tenon, ½ in. thick by 3 in. wide by 4 in. long

Bottom stretchers are bolted in place.

DOG HOLE DETAIL

1¼ in.

¼ in.

1 in.

92°

1 in.

BENCHDOG DETAIL

1⅛ in.

¾ in.

6 in.

¾ in.

2 in.

11⁄16 in.

Wooden spring is ⅛ in. thick and screwed to body of benchdog.

very large workpieces, with the vise jaw, leg, and edge of the bench providing a solid grip unmatched by other vises. However, to do so, the leg vise incorporates an adjustable "parallel guide" at the bottom that must be set to roughly the thickness of the workpiece with a removable pin. The extra step takes a little getting used to, but the results are well worth it. Benchcrafted will soon have a new version of the leg vise available, at a higher price, with a scissor mechanism that will eliminate this step.

At the right end, in place of a standard tail vise, is the wagon vise—basically a sliding block with a benchdog that rides in a slot in the top. The huge advantage of this style of vise is that while providing tenacious clamping action for workpieces on the benchtop, the wagon vise has no tail that can loosen up, sag, or vibrate. This makes a big difference in how secure your work feels on the bench. Also, when you've used a wagon vise for a while, you will no longer avoid using the front right section of your workbench—it will be just as firm and flat as the rest of the top. Suddenly, you have the whole bench at your disposal.

One thing you give up when you install a wagon vise is the ability to clamp very large

Three stage glue-up. Miller made the 21-in.-wide main section of the benchtop in three 7-in. subassemblies, giving him better control of the glue-ups. He used hand-screw clamps to keep the boards aligned (above).

Parts of the benchtop

Main section comprises three subassemblies.

Flatsawn boards glued face-to-face create a very stable quartersawn slab.

End cap

Dog-hole strip

First two boards in front subassembly are notched before glue-up to create recess for wagon vise.

Recess, 2⁵⁄₁₆ in. wide by 2¹⁄₁₆ in. deep by 16¾ in. long

Machining a major workpiece. Before gluing the three subassemblies together, Miller jointed them flat and square. He used infeed and outfeed supports to aid the process (right).

It's a cinch. The three subassemblies came together in the final glue-up of the main section of the benchtop (above). Clamps top and bottom evened out the pressure. Clamps on the ends aligned the sections.

and thick workpieces, such as bedposts, in the vertical position, the way you can with a traditional tail vise. The wagon vise gives you something in return, however: a slot in the benchtop where you can clamp tall boards up to 4 in. wide and 1¾ in. thick, for dovetailing, for example.

Although the Benchcrafted vise hardware does not come with printed instructions, there are excellent installation manuals on the manufacturer's website (which you can print out), along with a library of videos and a FAQ (frequently asked questions) section. The information they supply is so extensive and well presented that I've included just a few pointers about the vise installations in this chapter and instead focused on building the bench suited to these two superb vises.

Beefy top welcomes handwork

Weight is the key to a stable bench, especially one that will be used frequently for handplaning and chisel work, and in keeping with the uncompromising nature of the vises, I decided to make the top of the bench a solid slab 4 in. thick by 24 in. wide by 84 in. long—about 165 lb. of ash. After

Square dog holes made easy

Dado and rout. After plowing out most of the waste with a dado set, Miller used a jig and router with a rub collar to create the benchdog slots. Then he added a facing board to close off the holes.

DOG BOARD

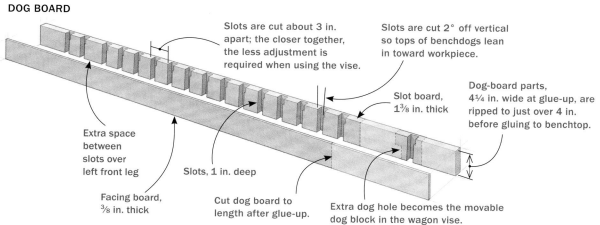

Slots are cut about 3 in. apart; the closer together, the less adjustment is required when using the vise.

Slots are cut 2° off vertical so tops of benchdogs lean in toward workpiece.

Slot board, 1⅜ in. thick

Dog-board parts, 4¼ in. wide at glue-up, are ripped to just over 4 in. before gluing to benchtop.

Extra space between slots over left front leg

Facing board, ⅜ in. thick

Slots, 1 in. deep

Cut dog board to length after glue-up.

Extra dog hole becomes the movable dog block in the wagon vise.

milling flatsawn 8/4 stock, I ripped boards a bit over 4 in. wide and stood them on edge to glue them together, giving me a very stable, quartersawn slab.

You could save some wood and make a portion of the top thinner. You can even hide that fact if you add an end cap to the leg vise end of the bench. But the weight and thickness are an advantage, helping keep the bench very stable even during aggressive work. And having a top of consistent thickness makes clamping down workpieces simpler.

The top has four main components: the main section, the dog-hole board, the face board, and the end cap. I started with the main section. At 4 in. thick by 21 in. wide by 7 ft. long, it is a beast. I decided to glue it up in three 7-in.-wide subassemblies to make the glue-ups more manageable.

Save the extra dog hole. When the glue was dry, Miller cut the dog board to length. He used the extra dog hole (right) to make the moveable dog block for the wagon vise. Then he glued the dog board to the benchtop and planed it flush.

One jig, two uses

Big crosscut, big tenon. Miller's cuff jig gives him perfectly aligned fences above and below. He used it to cut the benchtop to length with a circular saw (top), cutting halfway through from each face. Then he moved the jig and used it with a router (above) to cut the massive tenon that will mate with the end cap.

CUFF JIG

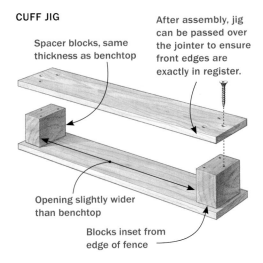

Spacer blocks, same thickness as benchtop

After assembly, jig can be passed over the jointer to ensure front edges are exactly in register.

Opening slightly wider than benchtop

Blocks inset from edge of fence

Even so, it helps to work with a glue that has an extended open time, so you have more than a few minutes to get each section assembled. To keep the boards in alignment during the glue-up, I used hand-screw clamps at either end, working from one side to the other and tweaking as necessary. I get a very flat result with this method, but if you're inclined you can cut biscuit joints to keep the boards in register—don't glue the biscuits, since they are just serving to ensure good alignment.

After the glue cured, I ran the three subassemblies through the jointer and planer and glued up the complete main section of the top. Again I used hand-screw clamps during the glue-up to bring the three sections into the same plane, but a few biscuits could perform the same function.

Creating the rest of the benchtop

The best way to make square dog holes is by routing slots across one board and gluing a thinner board to it. Before cutting the slots with a router jig, I wasted away most of the wood with a dado set on the tablesaw. Because the dog holes were to be 2° off vertical, I tacked a slightly angled temporary fence to the bed of a crosscut sled to make the dado cuts.

Gluing the slotted board to its facing piece is a little tricky. The boards are floppy, and should be glued against a flat surface—I used the main section of the top. Spread the glue carefully to avoid squeeze-out inside the dog holes. The end cap has a large mortise to accept the tenon on the right end of the benchtop. It's easy to rout the slot for the mortise using a plunge router and an auxiliary fence. To support the router throughout the cut, I left the end cap a few inches overlong on both ends.

Face board and end cap go on together.
Miller used the bandsaw (with a support stand to keep the long workpiece level) to cut the tails in the face board. The rabbet visible below the tails (above) provided better registration (right) when Miller marked the pins on the end cap from the tails.

Trim and tenon the top

I made a simple cuff jig that works both for cutting the bench to length with a circular saw and for milling the big tenon that will mate with the end cap. The jig provides fences across the top and bottom that are exactly in register. If you need to adjust the alignment of the fences after screwing the jig together, give it a pass over the jointer.

After cutting the bench to length, I used the cuff jig and a straight bit to rout the large tenon on the end of the top. I cut back both tenon ends with a handsaw and cleaned up the shoulder with a shoulder plane.

Then I put the end cap in place and marked and cut the back end of it flush to the back edge of the benchtop. To see where to cut the end cap at the front, I slid the face board in place and marked along its outside face.

Do the dovetails

Now I was ready to do the dovetailing. It's the signature bit of handwork on the bench, and for a little extra flair I chose to use double-dovetails—or hounds-tooth dovetails as they're called. They're an added challenge, but they provide more strength plus pizzazz.

A lot of chopping. Although Miller started excavating the pins with a trim router, most of the wood had to be removed by hand.

I cut the tails in the face board at the bandsaw with a support behind me to keep the 7-ft.-long board flat on the table. Using the bandsaw (vs. a handsaw) makes it easy to keep the sides of the tails square. I used the bandsaw to nibble away the waste between the tails, then cleaned up to the scribed base lines with a chisel. I cut away the waste to the outside of the tails on the tablesaw.

Dry-fit the end cap. The end cap is fitted to the tenon and bolted in place through oval clearance holes (left) to allow for seasonal movement of the top. With the cap in place, Miller used the Bench-crafted template to mark it for the wagon vise handle hardware (right); then he removed the end cap and took it to the drill press.

Glued and bolted. At final assembly, Miller bolted the end cap back onto the benchtop with no glue on the tenon. He glued the face board to the front of the top and to the end cap at the dovetail.

With the tails finished, I scribed the pins from them with a knife. I used a combination of hand sawing, routing, and chiseling to cut the half-blind pins. To clean out the waste, I worked the chisels in all directions—with the grain, against it, and across it.

Don't assemble yet

It's best to mark and drill the end cap for the wagon vise screw hardware before final assembly of the top. With the end cap bolted in place, I used the paper template provided by Benchcrafted to locate the holes, then unbolted the end cap and took it to the drill press.

Similarly, it's much easier and more accurate to drill the holes and rout the mortises in the left front leg and the leg vise's jaw before the base is assembled. All the holes are better cut at the drill press, and cutting the through-mortise for the parallel guide in the left front leg (which is 3 in. thick), if done with a router, requires working from both the inside and outside faces of the leg.

Mating the base to the benchtop

Because the leg vise relies on having the benchtop flush with the front face of the legs, the precise location of the benchtop on the base is essential. I used slip tenons in the tops of the legs to keep the base and top in

Installing the wagon vise

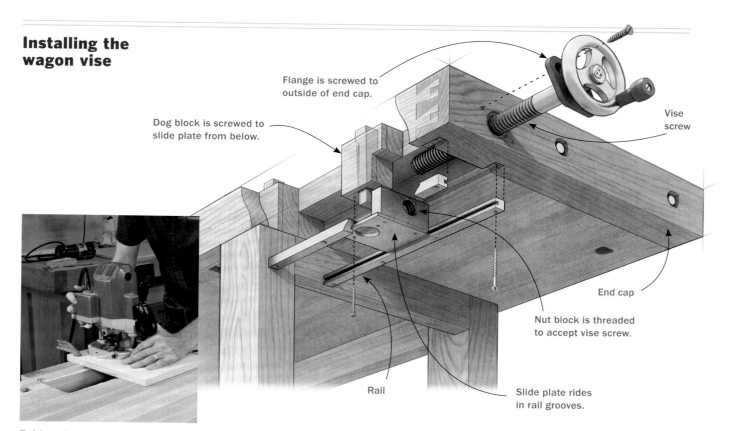

Flange is screwed to outside of end cap.

Dog block is screwed to slide plate from below.

Vise screw

Nut block is threaded to accept vise screw.

End cap

Rail

Slide plate rides in rail grooves.

Bridge the gap. A wide sub-base screwed to the router provided the support so Miller could rout accurate grooves for the two wagon vise rails, working with the benchtop upside down.

Two rails in one plane. To ensure that the wagon vise operates smoothly, its rails must be perfectly parallel and lie in the same plane.

Drop in the dog block. With the benchtop flipped right side up, Miller fitted the dog block into its slot and fastened it to the moving plate with a screw from below. The nut block reinforces it well in use.

Keys to a solid leg vise

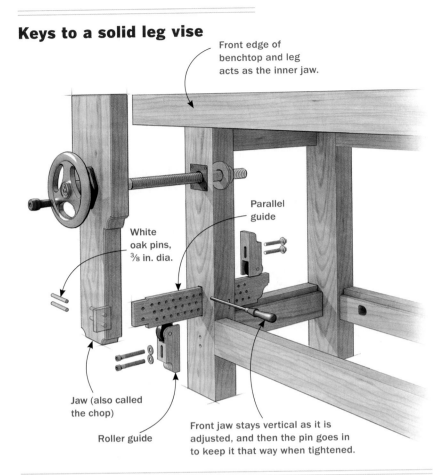

Front edge of benchtop and leg acts as the inner jaw.

Parallel guide

White oak pins, ⅜ in. dia.

Jaw (also called the chop)

Roller guide

Front jaw stays vertical as it is adjusted, and then the pin goes in to keep it that way when tightened.

register. I glued the tenons into the legs but left them dry in the top. Once the base was glued up, I inverted it on the underside of the benchtop and used squares and straightedges to locate it exactly. Then I scribed around the tenons and routed mating mortises in the underside of the top. I made the rear mortises oversize in length by ¼ in. to permit the top to expand and contract.

Final flattening

When it comes time to level and smooth the top of a bench, I do the job with handplanes. It takes some elbow grease, but it's not terribly difficult. If you're not inclined for the workout, you could always outsource the flattening to a shop with a thickness sander. Either way, it's an important step in the process. The flatter the benchtop, the better you'll like your bench, knowing that you can count on it as a reference surface.

I start by planing directly across the top at 90° to the grain direction. You could use winding sticks and straightedges to check

Drill before assembling the base. After using a Forstner bit to drill a hole through the leg-vise jaw for the vise screw, Miller used the same bit as a transfer punch to mark the front leg for drilling.

Base and top must be flush. For the leg vise to work properly, the front leg must be flush with the front of the benchtop. With the base aligned, Miller marked the position of the slip tenons in the leg tops so he could rout mating mortises in the benchtop.

your progress, but the planing itself gives plenty of indication of where the low and high spots are.

Then I switch to working the top at a 45° angle. I cover the top completely, then work it at 45° the other way. Lastly, I switch to planing with the grain, taking much lighter shavings for these final passes.

I want it dead flat, but I don't fuss about getting a furniture-quality surface. It's a workbench, after all, and I want to hurry up and put it and those two new vises to use.

Outfeed Table Doubles as a Workbench

KELLY J. DUNTON

I have a small shop on the second story of a barn. When I needed a new outfeed table for my tablesaw, I saw it as a chance to squeeze one more work surface into the small space. So I designed the outfeed table to double as a workbench. Made entirely of soft maple, the table has a hefty top with a large cast-iron vise. Mortise-and-tenon joinery, along with a few bridle joints, makes for a rigid base. Construction is not difficult. I'll show you how to build this table from the bottom to the top.

Make the base

Regardless of the technique you use (mortiser, router, or drill press and chisel), deep through-mortises like those in the trestle feet and posts of this table can be difficult to make. I get around all that work by cutting the mortises on the tablesaw.

Here's the wizardry behind my method. The feet and posts are made by gluing two pieces together, so I cut the joinery before assembling these parts. Start with the stretcher mortises in the posts. Mill the two halves of the post to their final dimensions. You only have to lay out the mortise location on one half of the post. Stop blocks on a miter gauge guide the work from there.

Put a dado set in your tablesaw—a ¾-in.-wide stack works well. Now attach a long auxiliary fence to your miter gauge. You'll need two stop blocks to control the mortise's width and location. To set the stop blocks,

Versatile and strong

Designed to carry at least twice its weight, this tablesaw outfeed bench has a base that can stand up to high-stress jobs like handplaning. And the joints are easy to make.

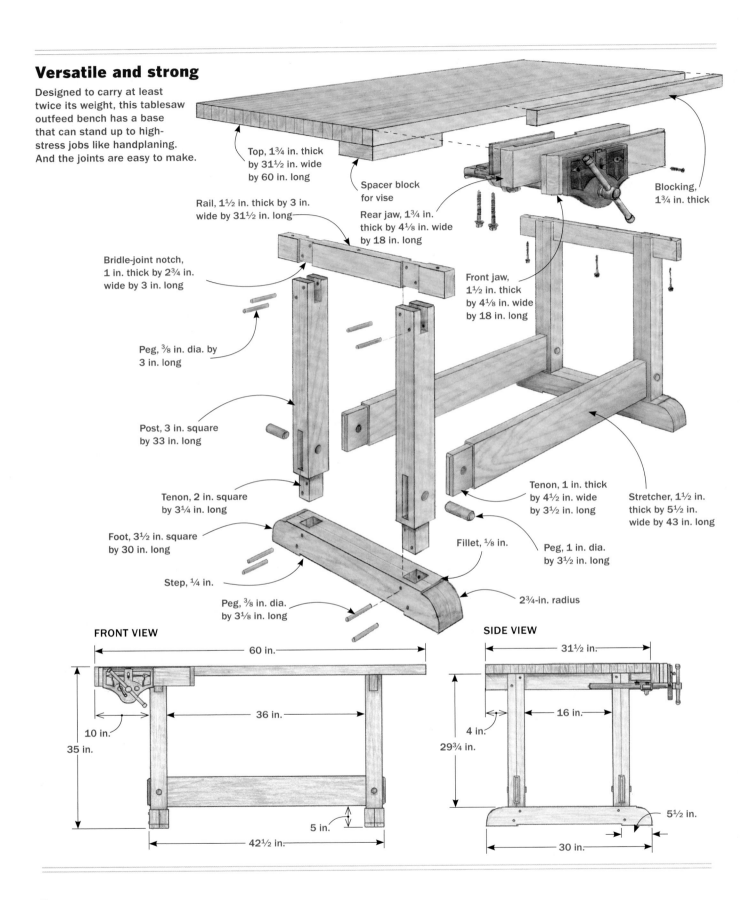

Top, 1¾ in. thick by 31½ in. wide by 60 in. long

Spacer block for vise

Rear jaw, 1¾ in. thick by 4⅛ in. wide by 18 in. long

Blocking, 1¾ in. thick

Rail, 1½ in. thick by 3 in. wide by 31½ in. long

Bridle-joint notch, 1 in. thick by 2¾ in. wide by 3 in. long

Front jaw, 1½ in. thick by 4⅛ in. wide by 18 in. long

Peg, ⅜ in. dia. by 3 in. long

Post, 3 in. square by 33 in. long

Tenon, 2 in. square by 3¼ in. long

Tenon, 1 in. thick by 4½ in. wide by 3½ in. long

Stretcher, 1½ in. thick by 5½ in. wide by 43 in. long

Foot, 3½ in. square by 30 in. long

Fillet, ⅛ in.

Peg, 1 in. dia. by 3½ in. long

Step, ¼ in.

2¾-in. radius

Peg, ⅜ in. dia. by 3⅛ in. long

FRONT VIEW

60 in.

36 in.

10 in.

35 in.

5 in.

42½ in.

SIDE VIEW

31½ in.

16 in.

4 in.

29¾ in.

5½ in.

30 in.

Cut mortises at the tablesaw. Gluing up the posts from two pieces of thinner stock allows you to cut the deep stretcher mortises at the tablesaw—a nifty trick.

Do the ends first. Stop blocks on the miter gauge fence ensure that the mortise's length and location will be the same on every post half. Hog out the waste between the ends. The ¾-in.-wide dado set eats through the meat of the mortise in just a few passes.

Clamp the halves together. A filler block in the mortise keeps the halves properly aligned, while a set of cauls keeps them aligned side to side. After the clamps are set, knock out the filler block.

Cut the tenons next. A stop block determines the length.

place the workpiece against this auxiliary fence and slide it to the right so that the left end of the mortise is aligned with the left side of the dado set. Clamp the block to the fence, snug against the right end of the post half. Slide the post back to the left until the right end of the mortise aligns with the right side of the dado set. Clamp the other stop block to the fence, tight against the left end of the post.

Cut one end of the mortise. Slide the post half against the other stop and cut the other end. Cut away the waste between these two cuts with the dado set. Repeat the process for the remaining mortises.

To keep the post halves properly aligned during the glue-up, I put a filler block in the mortise. It should be the same thickness and width as the mortise, but make it several inches longer so that you can knock it out after clamping the halves together. Don't leave it in while the glue dries.

Next up is the bridle joint at the top of each post that houses the rail. Start at the

Bridle joints for the trestle rails. The rails are long enough to support the top out to its edges. Cut the cheeks first. Set the fence to cut the cheek nearest to it. Flip the post over to make the second cheek cut to center the joint.

Clean out the waste, too. The bandsaw handles most of it, but you'll need to pare the baseline with a chisel.

Notch the stretchers. Use two stop blocks to control the notch's location and length. Leave the joint a bit thick, so you can plane it to fit the open mortise in the post.

bandsaw, cutting the cheeks and removing as much waste as you can with diagonal cuts down to the bottom corners. Clean up the remaining waste with a chisel.

Now make the feet. They also need mortises for the post tenons. Make them the same way as the stretcher mortises in the posts—on the tablesaw, before gluing the

halves together. After gluing up the feet, cut their profile at the bandsaw.

Now you're ready to drill all of the peg holes at the drill press. Most Forstner bits are too short to make it all the way through the posts and feet, so use a brad-point bit instead. Also, slide the filler block that you used to align the mortises during the glue-up back into the mortise before you drill the

Drawbore the Joints

The big advantage of the drawbored joint is that the peg pulls the tenon shoulders tight to the posts, helping to create a rigid and strong assembly without the need for clamps.

As peg is driven through the joint, it pulls the holes into alignment, which pulls the shoulder tighter against the post.

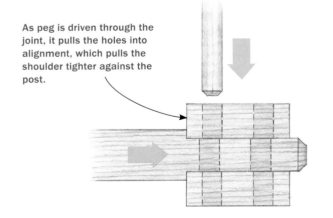

Transfer the hole. Use the same bit you used to drill the peg holes. Just give it a tap.

Offset the mark. Use a punch to move it slightly (1/32 in.) closer to the shoulder.

Now drill. Any movement during drilling can prevent the drawbore from working properly, so clamp the post to the drill-press table.

hole. This prevents the bit from blowing out the grain inside the mortise.

With all of the mortises completed, begin the tenons. I cut all of the tenons at the tablesaw with a dado set and miter gauge, using a stop block to ensure consistent shoulders. I do the tenons at the bottom of the posts first.

Next up are the stretchers and rails. The stretchers have through-tenons that stick out 1/2 in. beyond the post. After fitting the tenons, cut them to length and chamfer the ends with a block plane.

The end rails are notched on both faces to fit into the bridle joints. Cut the notches

with a dado set. After fitting the joints, I chamfer the ends of the rails with a block plane.

No clamps needed for assembly

Now that all of the joinery is cut, you can assemble the base. Start with the trestle ends. Its joints are glued, but they are also drawbored—including the bridle joints—to ensure that the tenon shoulder is pulled tight. To set up the joint for drawboring, dry-fit the tenon in the mortise. Now grab the bit you used to drill the peg holes. Slip it into the hole and give it a light tap, just enough to mark the tenon. Pull apart the joint and use the punch to offset the mark about 1/32 in. closer to the shoulder. Drill a hole through the tenon at this new mark.

Spread glue on the joint, insert the tenon, and drive the peg into the hole. As it passes through the hole, the peg forces the tenon deeper into the mortise and pulls the shoulder tight against the post. No need for clamps.

After the end assemblies are together, connect them with the two long stretchers. These don't get glue, so just put them together and knock in the drawbore pegs. Just like that, the base is done. Now on to the top.

Make the top and install the vise

The top is laminated from strips of maple. This means you'll need plenty of glue and a bunch of clamps. To avoid a lot of flattening after the glue-up, I use a proven technique that ensures a dead-flat top. Glue up several sections of the top first. Each section needs to be narrow enough to fit across your jointer and through your planer after the glue has dried. Because I have a 12-in. jointer and planer, that means three sections. If your machines are smaller, you'll need to break the top into more sections.

Assemble the base. Drawbored joinery means no clamps are needed. Once the base is together, make and attach the top.

Posts and feet first. After spreading glue on the joint, slide the post into the mortise. Because the peg hole in the tenon is offset toward the shoulder, the tenon is pulled into the mortise and against the shoulder when you knock in the pegs.

No glue for the long stretchers. Slide the tenons in dry (left), then knock in the big drawbore pegs (above). This joint won't work loose, but you'll still be able to take it apart should you need to move the bench.

After the sections have been rejointed (including edge jointing) and planed, glue them all together at once. Take care to ensure that they're aligned end to end and top to bottom. Doing this carefully should eliminate any need for flattening afterward.

To install the vise, you'll need to attach a spacer block between the bench and the vise to position the top edge of the vise's rear jaw flush with the top surface. This makes the vise much more useful for cutting joinery and planing boards on edge. Now mill up a piece of maple that's as thick as the rear jaw, as wide as the top is thick, and long enough to run from the vise to the opposite end of the bench. Glue it to the benchtop. This brings the benchtop in line with the vise's rear jaw and makes clamping boards in the vise much easier.

Big top, less work. Glue up the top in sections small enough to joint and plane, then glue those sections together to complete the top.

Square up, then glue up. After jointing a face, run the sections through the planer (top), then joint the edges square to the faces. A caul across the width and clamps over the gluelines at the ends keep the three sections aligned (above).

Rout clearance slots. At 5 in. to 6 in. long (depending on the miter gauge you use) and just wider than the slots in your saw's table, these give miter bars a place to go so that workpieces can clear the back of the blade.

Bolt on the vise. Cast-iron vises are strong and easy to install, but their metal jaws can mar and damage workpieces, so cover them with thick, shopmade wooden jaws. A spacer block (above) lowers the vise so that the top edge of the back jaw sits just below the surface of the bench.

Spacer Block Positions Jaws

Size the block so that the vise jaws sit just below the benchtop after installation. This way, you don't have to worry about accidentally hitting them with a plane or saw.

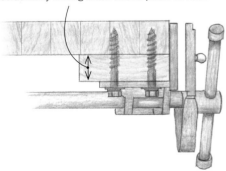

Add the rear jaw. Notch it to fit over the metal jaw. Screw through it and the holes in the metal jaw to anchor the screws in the benchtop.

Block out the top. This brings the front edge in line with the wooden rear jaw, which makes it easier to clamp wide and long boards in the vise.

Put the top on the base. Attach it with six lag screws, three at each end. Put the table in place behind your tablesaw. Mark where the miter slots in the saw's table hit the benchtop, then widen it just a bit. Slide the table away from the saw, and rout slots in the benchtop to create clearance for miter bars. I do this with a flush-trimming bit and a template that has a notch slightly wider than the miter-gauge slot in the tablesaw.

Now the table is done. Apply some oil to the base and top, slide it into place, and get to work.

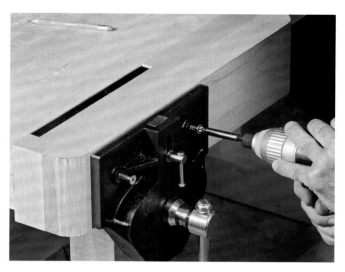

The front jaw is last. After screwing it in place, plane the top edge of the wooden jaws flush to the benchtop.

Don't Build a New Workbench

CHRISTOPHER SCHWARZ

A new workbench—with tons of mass and new vises—is a tempting idea when you're struggling with an inherited or entry-level bench. If you love building workbenches, go ahead and build the bench of your dreams. But if you prefer building furniture, there are a dozen inexpensive or free ways to improve any existing bench.

Most of these improvements involve only a few scraps of wood and metal—and rethinking what a good working bench should look like.

End the wobble

Many entry-level benches sway during heavy planing or sawing. This swaying makes you work harder and reduces your accuracy when sawing. If the bench is bolted together,

Create a sturdy stance

Address the top-to-base connection, eliminate racking, and immobilize the base.

Lock the top to the base. Gravity isn't enough to hold the top to the base. Use carriage bolts (left) for a strong connection between the two.

Plywood panels stop the racking. Instantly improve a lightweight bench by adding a plywood panel or two to the base, turning a frame into a solid box. A diagonal clamp squares the base for screwing.

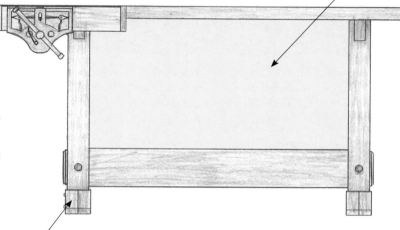

first tighten all its bolts. Then try these two improvements.

Improve the connection between the benchtop and its base. Usually the benchtop is held in place with gravity and maybe a couple of lag screws. This is not enough. Bolt the top to the base using carriage bolts (two bolts at each end), washers, and nuts. Countersink the heads of the bolts into the benchtop well below the working surface. To stop the base from swaying, glue and screw a wide piece of ¾-in. plywood to the rear of the base. If that doesn't do the trick, add a similar piece to the front of the base.

Immobilize the base

Even the beefiest workbench can slide across the floor during heavy handplaning. Lock the bench in place on the floor with cleats. Screw or nail them to the floor on the inside or outside of the legs.

If cleats alone don't do the trick, drive lag screws up through the floorboards into the legs to immobilize a jumpy workbench. If your workbench has sled feet you can drive the lag screws from above.

Eliminate slide. Surround the feet with cleats that are nailed or screwed to the floor. The cleats can be positioned on the inside or outside of the workbench's legs. Cleats on the outside are easier to install; cleats on the inside are less likely to trip you.

Bolt it down. If cleats alone don't do the trick, drive lag screws up through the floorboards. If your workbench has sled feet, you can drive the screws from above.

Block out the legs if you have to. On benches with trestle-style bases, you can still create a flush clamping surface by blocking out the front leg flush with the benchtop. The benefit of this method is that you can predrill the block before mounting it.

Put the legs to work. Remounting the benchtop or blocking out the legs flush with the front edge gives you options to add support for clamping large parts. On benches with straight legs, it's easy to reposition the base so that the front legs are flush with the front edge of the benchtop.

Add holes for support pegs. Drill holes through the legs for pegs or holdfasts, which are handy for supporting long boards or panels when clamped in the front vise.

Put the legs to work

The front legs of your workbench can become clamping surfaces if you bring them in line with the front edge of the benchtop. This is handy when planing the edges of large doors or panels.

You can bring the legs in line with the benchtop by shifting the base forward and bolting it in place there, or you can glue blocks of wood to the front legs to fill the space and accomplish the same goal.

Improve the grip of vises

Most vises grip the work with contact surfaces that are metal, which can mar the workpiece, or wood, which is slippery. I prefer to line vise jaws with a grippy material, which can make any old vise work like new.

I've tried different materials, from suede to cork to neoprene. My favorite material is

Big jobs aren't a problem. With the front leg flush with the benchtop, you can use a round peg or holdfast to support the bottom of the workpiece. This allows you to work on big parts like tabletops or even full-size doors.

TIP Give your vise more grip. A leather or rubber liner adds grip while protecting the workpiece. Adhere the liner to one side at a time, using waxed paper to protect the opposite face from glue. A spacer block of soft pine helps distribute the clamping pressure evenly while the glue (contact adhesive or epoxy) cures.

Crubber, a durable and grippy mix of rubber and cork available from Benchcrafted.

Workholding with no end vise

Until the 14th century, most woodworking benches didn't use vises, and you don't need them, either.

You can use a single-point planing stop. This square stick of wood (3 in. square by 12 in. long is a typical size) is friction-fitted into a mortise right through the benchtop. Adjust the stop up and down with mallet taps. To improve its grip, many stops have a blacksmith-made fitting that's toothed across the front. But it's also common to find plan-

Securing work. There are infinite ways to get creative about holding your work, from single-point stops to clamps and holdfasts. Figure out what you need to clamp. Then get your own system going.

Single-point stop. Very common in old benches, these planing stops have teeth that improve their grip. The points will mark the end grain of your boards, but tool marks like these are common on antiques. Embrace them.

Add a batten for wide stock. Sometimes a screw or two can solve the trickiest workholding problem. If you don't have a holdfast, just screw the batten in place. You won't be the first—or the last—to do it. (It's a workbench, not an altar.)

Holdfasts. While you can do without a holdfast, they are very handy and versatile. A quick whack on the top of the crook tightens it in place. Then a whack on the back of the crook loosens it.

A holdfast's helper. A notched board, called a doe's foot, can stop spinning and control the back end of your work, allowing you to plane wide boards against a planing stop.

Holdfasts, a planing stop, and a sticking board. When planing thin moldings, the work wants to bend. A sticking board against a planing stop, secured to the benchtop with holdfasts, fixes that problem.

ing stops that have teeth made from old nails driven through the stop.

Once you have a planing stop, you can make a couple of additions that will eliminate the need for an end vise or tail vise and solve the problem of pinching a workpiece between dogs, which can slow your work and, worse, bend your workpiece.

First you need a pair of holdfasts. The Gramercy Tools holdfasts are inexpensive

(around $30 at Tools for Working Wood) and work well.

In addition to holding your work directly to the benchtop, holdfasts can secure sticking boards, battens, and a "doe's foot" to eliminate the need for an end vise.

The doe's foot is the simplest and most ingenious of these devices. Press the end of your work hard into the teeth in your planing stop. Put the notch of the doe's foot on

Vise alternatives. Clamps, hooks, and notches are excellent vise alternatives. Even without vises you can dovetail, cut tenons, and shape your work. For dovetails use bar clamps across the top of your bench to hold workpieces vertically against the front of the bench. It's not much slower than a dedicated vise.

Crochet, or hook, is an effective end stop. With the workpiece resting on pegs in the legs and the front end nestled into the crochet, you don't need clamps to edge-plane a long board.

An almost-forgotten way to cut tenons. These notches show up on lots of old benches, with origins from Italy to an Ohio Shaker community. Rest the workpiece in the notch, and tap in a wedge (only 1° or 2° slope is necessary) to lock it in place. It helps to have a selection of wedges for different sizes of work.

the back corner of your work. Fasten the doe's foot with a holdfast.

Holdfasts are also useful for securing a batten across the end of the benchtop for planing (or sanding) wide carcase sides. Place one end of the batten against the planing stop. Secure the other end with a holdfast. Now you can easily plane the side of a carcase without vises or additional clamps.

If you aren't willing to buy holdfasts, there's a cheaper solution: Screw the doe's foot, sticking board, or batten to the benchtop. I use drywall screws.

No front vise?

If you don't have a front vise, or one that holds well, there are several ways around the problem. If you need to dovetail a drawer or a case side, clamp it to the front edge of the benchtop with bar clamps.

Hand-sawing tenons can be tricky without a front vise, but there is a workaround for this problem, too. Some old benches had a large square notch cut into the edge or end of the benchtop, and work was secured in the notch with the help of a softwood wedge.

For edge-planing long boards, you can use a crochet. In France in particular, woodworkers would use the crochet—French for "hook"—to secure work against the front edge of the benchtop. The crochet is indeed a hook, and you can push work into it to plane boards on edge with the help of a clamp or holdfast to hold the board's far end.

Hand screws. A pair of heavy hand-screw clamps are as useful as a holdfast. Hand screws are a valuable yet often forgotten tool in the modern workshop. Use them as a dovetail vise. With your workpiece against the front of the bench, use hand screws on both sides to hold the piece. Then clamp the hand screws to the top of the bench with bar clamps.

Hand screw holds little pieces. Use the hand screw to grab a small workpiece, and then clamp the hand screw to the front of the bench to keep it all in place.

Two ways to edge-joint with a hand screw. For short pieces (left) clamp the workpiece in the hand screw, and then clamp the hand screw to the bench. For longer pieces (right), butt the front of the workpiece up to a stop and stabilize the back end with a hand screw.

Never underestimate the power of hand screws

These early clamps can be pressed into service for many operations: to make a face vise, to make a vise for dovetailing, as a planing stop, or as a small vise to hold odd-shaped things.

In fact, whenever I get stuck trying to hold a weird piece of work, I think: Could a hand screw fix this intractable problem? I'm surprised by how often the answer is yes.

And that's the funny thing about workholding. Throwing money at the problem doesn't always win the day. Most things can be held at any workbench by investing in only gravity, friction, wedges—and the occasional hand screw.

Rethinking the Workbench

Although the tablesaw is often cited as the center of the workshop, the workbench is where most of the action happens. For sharpening, handwork, sanding, assembling, and finishing, everyone needs a flat, solid surface to work on. But workbenches vary widely, as do the myriad ways that woodworkers accessorize them.

This special collection of ideas from readers of *Fine Woodworking* centers on the workbench, from the surface itself to everything that happens there.

Whether you are dreaming up a new bench or looking to improve the one you have, you are likely to find some great ideas here to make your bench work harder.

Use a glulam beam to make a flat, forgiving benchtop

While builders were constructing a combined garage and workshop at my house, I was building my first workbench. Looking closely at the laminated beams they were using, I saw my first benchtop. I went to the local lumberyard and purchased a 6-ft.-long portion of a laminated beam designed for interior use. It was much less expensive than purchasing similar lumber for laminating the top myself, not to mention the many hours of labor saved. While various dimensions are available, including widths up to 24 in., my beam/benchtop is 14 in. wide and 3½ in. thick. Adding a tool tray is an easy way to expand the width. While most glulam beams are softwood, I don't mind the nicks and dents it collects, plus I like the forgiving nature of the surface.

—*Peter Miller, Little Rock, Ark.*

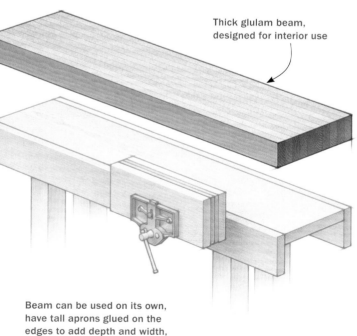

Thick glulam beam, designed for interior use

Beam can be used on its own, have tall aprons glued on the edges to add depth and width, or sit on a subtop as shown here.

Simple, solid box helps with handwork

I'm new to dovetailing, and before I made a grand investment in a leg vise or Moxon vise, I decided to try my own home brew. I made this simple but effective jig with scraps of particleboard and some wood strips. The four pieces of particleboard form a basic box, with one side left long to hang down and register the jig against the front of the bench. I glued wood strips along the front edge of the two working faces of the box. A couple of C-clamps attach the box to the bench.

Once I had built the jig, I found it useful for all sorts of hand-tool operations. To clamp a workpiece vertically for dovetailing or tenoning, for example, you just push the workpiece against the molding strip and secure it in seconds with Quick-Grip clamps. The workpiece is perfectly vertical and extremely stable.

Dumbbell bars create a cheap Moxon vise

I've been wanting a Moxon vise but have hesitated to spend the money on some of the beautiful Moxon hardware out there. I'm not crazy about the makeshift alternatives I've seen either. Stumbling around in the garage one day, I saw some discarded dumbbell bars with acme threading and large lock collars on the ends and thought how similar they were to twin-screw hardware. After 15 minutes at the bench grinder, removing one of the weight-plate stops on each bar, I had my hardware. I made some simple spacers and then made the vise jaws as you would for any Moxon vise. The jaws will open to about 3 in. and hold tightly and securely, even at 24 in. long. The nuts spin freely and with a little momentum will close on the fly just like the high-priced version. The dumbbell bars sell for about $20 on the web but are a dime a dozen at thrift stores and on Craigslist, etc. With a bit more work and creativity, I think the dumbbell bars will also work for a leg vise and other workbench fixtures.

—Rex Bostrom, Sweet Home, Ore.

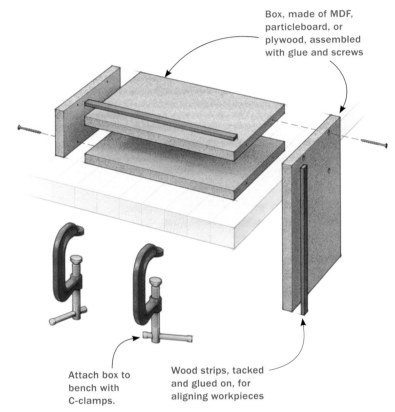

Box, made of MDF, particleboard, or plywood, assembled with glue and screws

Attach box to bench with C-clamps.

Wood strips, tacked and glued on, for aligning workpieces

It works just as well for clamping pieces horizontally, for chopping dovetails or routing, bringing the action to a more comfortable height in the process. And it really shines when lining up a tails board with a pins board to transfer the layout from one to the other.

—Steve Farnow, San Diego, Calif.

Easy way to divide and organize drawers

I build a lot of drawers in my shop to store all my wonderful tools, including under my workbench. But a drawerful of tools and supplies will become a mess in no time without some kind of organizer. I keep the entropy at bay with a simple system of custom dividers, held in place with hot-melt glue. I use ¼-in. plywood, which is cheap and easily cut to lengths and heights convenient for every application. The hot glue goes on fast and lets you start loading the drawer in seconds. Any time an adjustment is needed, a little bit of force will break the divider out. Fast, cheap, strong enough to serve, yet weak enough to remove without damage—it's perfect!

—*Chase Hansel, Melbourne, Fla.*

Plywood spacers seat against weight stop at rear and support rear jaw.

Threaded dumbbell bar, with weight stop ground off front end

Jaws, solid hardwood, milled straight and square, at least 24 in. long

Rear jaw is 2 in. longer at each end, with large hole for clamping.

Dumbbell nuts tighten front jaw on workpiece.

Carver's clamp allows access from all sides

I carve all sorts of objects, including some recent tuataras (a New Zealand lizard; see photo bottom left) in tough black beech burl. This simple bench clamp works for most of them, letting me attack the work from almost any angle and reposition the blank within seconds. The post attaches to the carving with yellow glue and is clamped in the two halves of a holding block, with force provided by any workbench vise. (You can add screws to strengthen the joint, but I haven't found that necessary in most cases.) Release the vise and the workpiece can be turned 360°; by tilting the holding block in the vise, you can angle the workpiece up to 30° to allow undercutting. Tighten the vise handle again, and the carving is rock solid.

You'll need a lathe to turn the post, but the rest of the construction is simple. You could turn the post from one block, but for a long-grain glue joint with the carving, I cut disks on the bandsaw to about 3½ in. dia., glued them in a stack, and turned the post from that. In fact, I turned a few posts, sized for various carvings. I counterbore and drill the posts for screws as needed. To make the holding block, I just traced the post on two pieces of 2x4 lumber and bandsawed the matching half-circles. After carving, you can remove the post from the workpiece with a handsaw and clean up the cut faces with a sander.

—*John Fry, Richmond, New Zealand*

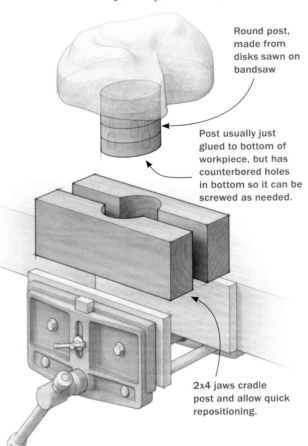

Round post, made from disks sawn on bandsaw

Post usually just glued to bottom of workpiece, but has counterbored holes in bottom so it can be screwed as needed.

2x4 jaws cradle post and allow quick repositioning.

Turn your workbench into a wide jointer

I came across some rough 16-in.-wide walnut boards, far too big for my jointer. Inspired by the jig Nick Offerman uses to surface big slabs (featured in *Fine Woodworking* issue 222), I created a simplified version that sets up in minutes, with simple boards that are jointed straight and attached to the front and back edge of my workbench, and a slightly simplified version of Offerman's sled.

The rear board is attached permanently with bolts and clamp handles, and it takes just a few seconds to raise. I clamp a second board to the front and measure to be sure the ends of both boards are the same height off the bench. My benchdogs make it easy to lock the lumber in place, and I wedge under the board, if necessary, to keep it level and stable. Then, just like Offerman, I load a fat straight bit in the router, zip the router back and forth on the sled, and the wide board comes out dead flat. If it will fit in my planer at that point, I surface the other side that way; if not, I just flip the board and use the jig again. On my bench I can flatten anything up to 25 in. wide and 6 ft. long.

—*Joshua Csehak, Boston, Mass.*

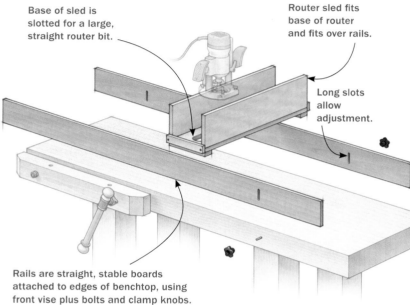

Base of sled is slotted for a large, straight router bit.

Router sled fits base of router and fits over rails.

Long slots allow adjustment.

Rails are straight, stable boards attached to edges of benchtop, using front vise plus bolts and clamp knobs.

DIY benchdogs work perfectly

Most shopmade benchdogs employ bullet-catch hardware or spring steel to create some friction in the dog hole so that they can be adjusted up and down without dropping out of reach. I found an easier answer for my benchdogs. I used rubber spline material left over from repairing window screens, setting it in a sawkerf to create the perfect amount of friction. I started with a dowel that was ¾ in. dia. (the same as my dog holes) by 3 ft. long, using the extra length as a way to keep a safe, firm grip on the dowel. A standard-kerf (0.125 in.) blade worked perfectly for the spline material. I cut the slot to a depth between ³⁄₃₂ in. and ⅛ in., pushing the first 7 in. of the dowel over the blade, trapped between the rip fence and a featherboard, with a zero-clearance insert below. Then I tilted the dowel up out of the cut. Last, I sawed the little notch at the tip of the dog, cut it to length, and tapped the spline into place with a hammer.

—*Adam Wagner, Plymouth, Mich.*

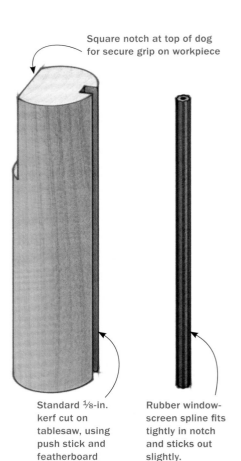

Square notch at top of dog for secure grip on workpiece

Standard ⅛-in. kerf cut on tablesaw, using push stick and featherboard

Rubber window-screen spline fits tightly in notch and sticks out slightly.

Metal scoop helps you sort through small parts

Here is a gadget I put together the other day that I should have made years ago. I am always sorting through nails, screws, nuts, and bolts, and I'm tired of dumping them out on the bench, losing some off the edge or down a dog hole, and then having to round them up afterward. It's a tedious, awkward process. This simple shopmade scoop is both tray and funnel, helping me fan out small parts for a closer look and then dump them smoothly back into the container they belong in. You might already have the materials you need. Any piece of stiff sheet metal will work, with a cheap door handle. The scoop is 12 in. long by 7 in. wide at the big end and 1½ in. wide at the funnel end. The sides taper from 3 in. high at the funnel end to ½ in. at the back. It sure speeds things up in my shop.

—*Neil Long, Mound City, Mo.*

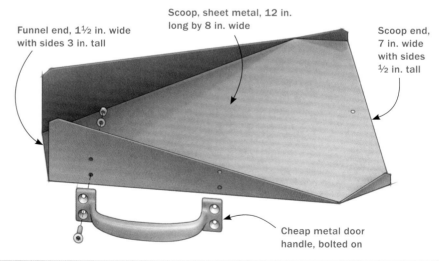

Funnel end, 1½ in. wide with sides 3 in. tall

Scoop, sheet metal, 12 in. long by 8 in. wide

Scoop end, 7 in. wide with sides ½ in. tall

Cheap metal door handle, bolted on

Work at the Right Height

CHRISTIAN BECKSVOORT

Everybody has an optimum height for their workbench. Standard benches are usually 36 in. tall, but some folks prefer one that's a bit shorter or taller, depending on their own size. The rule of thumb is that the bench should come up to about your wrist. That's great for 90% of all bench work, but it's not perfect for every operation. For example, planing requires more upper body strength, so a lower bench is better. Jobs like carving or sawing dovetails are both easier on your back if the bench is higher.

I have two methods for making my bench higher or lower, and as a result more user-friendly. With a little up-front work, both are quick to implement. I have a platform that lives under the bench that I can pull out and stand on in a minute. I also have an auxiliary

Medium, high, or low? Standard workbench height is great for most hand- and power-tool tasks, but sometimes it pays to gain a higher stance or to elevate the workpiece.

Is your bench comfortably sized for common tasks?

If you stand next to your bench with your arms at your sides, the top should be at wrist height. This general rule should see you through most tasks at the bench—chiseling, belt-sanding, planing, layout, marking, drawing, etc. My bench, like its owner, is on the tall side.

bench that I keep close at hand; when I want to do some high work I simply lift it up, clamp it in place, and get to it.

Both add-ons to my main bench have made me a more comfortable and efficient woodworker.

Lower bench puts you on top of the work

My workbench is 39 in. tall, which is great for the vast majority of my work, even a lot of planing tasks. However, when I need to plane or flatten an entire panel or when I want to

Tucked away until you need it. Becksvoort built a platform to store perfectly between the legs of his bench. Limited by the clearance beneath the bottom rail of the bench, Becksvoort added a lift system under the platform. Once he pulls the platform out, he can add to its height by folding down hinged risers.

More height means more power. The platform allows Becksvoort to work at a height that's most effective and ergonomic for planing a wide panel.

sand or plane tabletops or large panels held vertically in the vise, a lower bench surface would really help. Since I can't make my bench lower, I keep a 2¾ in. platform under it, fitted between the legs. I pull it out and stand on it, giving me a work surface that's effectively 36¼ in. high. If that's still too high, the platform has two hinged 3-in.-wide boards underneath that I can brace open with long spinners. Fold them down and the bench is 35 in. high, and I can really get into my work.

When returning it to its home under the bench, I found that the platform tended to bind if not pushed in straight. So I added strips between the legs to assure that the platform slides in straight. If you have a European-style bench with sled feet, the guide strips won't be necessary. If you want a platform the full length of your bench, you'll have to store it elsewhere. The platform can be made out of leftovers or cheap wood and can be built in just over an hour. It's an hour well spent, since it will make your work much easier. I also included a small nylon handle to make the platform easy to pull out.

A benchtop bench puts the work where you need it

Making a higher work surface can be more complex, but it's worth the effort since it greatly improves the ergonomics of sawing tails and pins for case sides, and of letter carving. Unlike planing, which usually takes 5 to 10 minutes, carving can last for hours. Spending that much time hunched over is tough on your back. The high surface is also useful for fussy jobs such as inlay, where you need to be close to the work.

I have a 12-in.-high auxiliary bench that I clamp to my workbench. Its top surface is 51 in. off the floor, so I can rest my arms comfortably on it, and it is perfect for carving. No more backaches. The front edge has a 24-in. Lie-Nielsen chain-driven vise. That makes it easy to clamp case sides for sawing dovetails. The vise doesn't rack, since both spindles turn at the same consistent rate. The 12-in., 18-in., and 24-in. vise hardware is all priced the same, so go for the big one.

You really don't need an auxiliary bench as complex as mine, and you may not need the full 12-in. height. Use your imagination to come up with a solution that satisfies you.

Bring the work up. With the smaller bench clamped to the main bench, Becksvoort can work at a level that will be comfortable for extended periods of time and allow him to use his body position productively.

You can buy a variety of vises and carving tops suitable for auxiliary benchtop benches from Lee Valley, Tools for Working Wood, and Lie-Nielsen. You also can get some guidance from Steve Latta ("Minibench Works Wonders," pp. 113–118) and Jeff Miller ("A Benchtop Bench," *Fine Woodworking* #176).

Same features as the main bench. By adding a vise to the auxiliary bench, Becksvoort keeps his usual methods intact while working at the optimal height.

Under-Bench Tool Storage

CHRISTIAN BECKSVOORT

The shelf below my workbench was always heaped with stray stuff—clamps, power cords, glue, scraps, jigs—things I often needed at the bench but never quite found a home for. It was constantly a mess, and the space above the mound of stuff was wasted, too. Sound familiar? Wouldn't a storage cabinet under there be just the ticket?

All it takes is proper planning and a little effort to create a custom cabinet to fit your bench, your tools, and your work style. Just as I did when building my wall-hung tool cabinet (featured in *Fine Woodworking* issue 153), I measured and grouped similar items to fit specific drawers beforehand to achieve an efficient and well-planned layout. Your cabinet will differ in size and layout, of course, depending on your bench and your tools.

Under-Bench Cabinet

Plywood and dadoes make for a quick, practical carcase; a cherry face frame and frame-and-panel back dress it up.

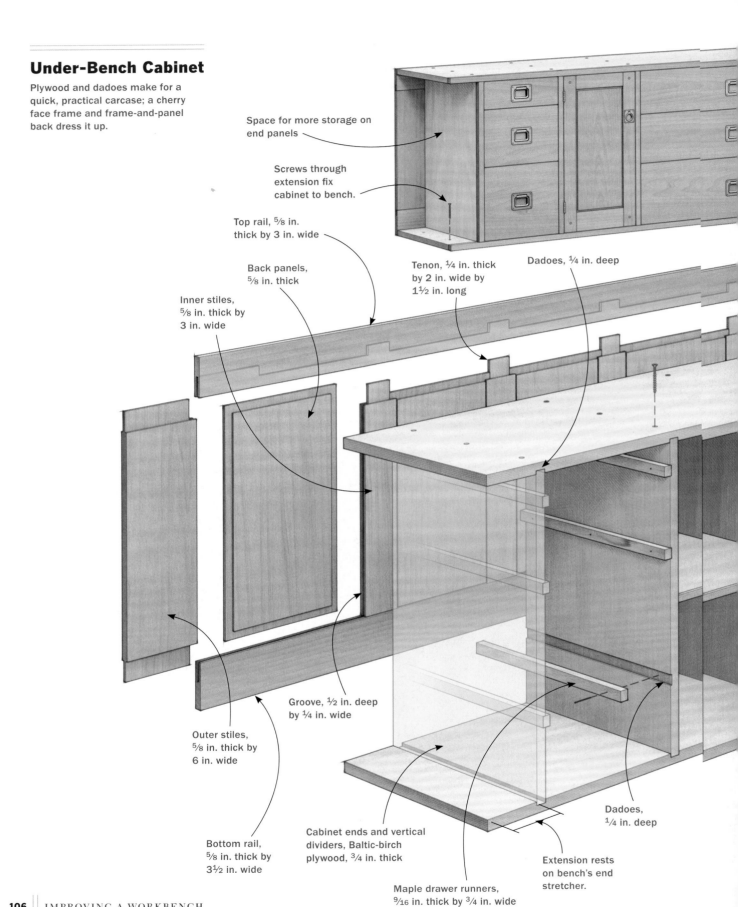

Space for more storage on end panels

Screws through extension fix cabinet to bench.

Top rail, 5/8 in. thick by 3 in. wide

Back panels, 5/8 in. thick

Inner stiles, 5/8 in. thick by 3 in. wide

Tenon, 1/4 in. thick by 2 in. wide by 1 1/2 in. long

Dadoes, 1/4 in. deep

Groove, 1/2 in. deep by 1/4 in. wide

Outer stiles, 5/8 in. thick by 6 in. wide

Bottom rail, 5/8 in. thick by 3 1/2 in. wide

Cabinet ends and vertical dividers, Baltic-birch plywood, 3/4 in. thick

Maple drawer runners, 9/16 in. thick by 3/4 in. wide

Dadoes, 1/4 in. deep

Extension rests on bench's end stretcher.

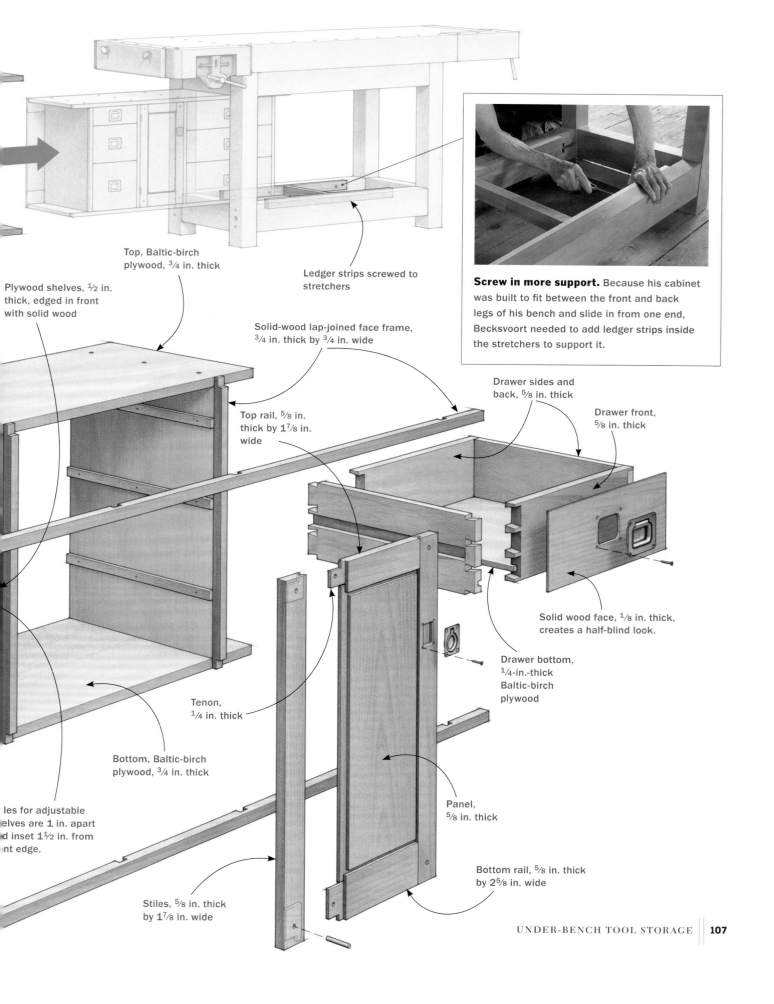

Top, Baltic-birch plywood, ³/₄ in. thick

Plywood shelves, ½ in. thick, edged in front with solid wood

Ledger strips screwed to stretchers

Solid-wood lap-joined face frame, ³/₄ in. thick by ³/₄ in. wide

Screw in more support. Because his cabinet was built to fit between the front and back legs of his bench and slide in from one end, Becksvoort needed to add ledger strips inside the stretchers to support it.

Drawer sides and back, ⁵/₈ in. thick

Drawer front, ⁵/₈ in. thick

Top rail, ⁵/₈ in. thick by 1⁷/₈ in. wide

Solid wood face, ¹/₈ in. thick, creates a half-blind look.

Tenon, ¹/₄ in. thick

Drawer bottom, ¹/₄-in.-thick Baltic-birch plywood

Bottom, Baltic-birch plywood, ³/₄ in. thick

Panel, ⁵/₈ in. thick

les for adjustable elves are 1 in. apart d inset 1½ in. from nt edge.

Stiles, ⁵/₈ in. thick by 1⁷/₈ in. wide

Bottom rail, ⁵/₈ in. thick by 2⁵/₈ in. wide

Layout Tips for Tools

Not every bench is the same, so you'll have to custom-fit this design to suit your situation. To determine the exterior dimensions of your cabinet, measure the distance between the legs of your workbench. My cabinet slides in from the end of the bench, just fitting between the front and rear legs, and leaving a 3-in.-wide clamping ledge along both the front and back of the bench. This also keeps the cabinet from interfering with the benchdogs. If your bench doesn't have stretchers positioned to support the cabinet, you may have to add ledger strips as I did.

Some time spent planning the arrangement of items in the drawers and cabinet will result in the most efficient layout. I started by grouping similar items that might go into the same drawer. I put all the stuff that accumulates in the tool well—sanding blocks, glue bottles, pencils, tape, spacers, and partially used sandpaper—together in the top shallow drawer. Larger items like clamps, hold-downs, and bench hooks fit in the larger drawers.

When I designed my wall-hung tool cabinet I made scaled graph-paper cutouts of my tools to find the best fit. But here I simply laid things out on the bench to see how they fit together. I cut a scrap to the length of the cabinet, arranged the tools, and marked the door and drawer sizes on the stick.

Plywood case and simple joinery

Since this is a shop project, I used plywood for the carcase, cut simple dado joints, and screwed it together. But I dressed it up with a solid face frame in front and a frame-and-panel back. When you cut the plywood to size, subtract ¾ in. from the width for the face frame and ⅝ in. for the paneled back. Cut out the shelves at the same time, subtracting ¼ in. for solid lipping on the front edge.

At the tablesaw, use the dado set to cut dadoes in the top and bottom for the dividers and in the ends and vertical dividers to accept the runners for the side-hung drawers. Then glue and screw the case together. The screws are driven from the top and bottom, so they won't show. With the case assembled,

drill holes for adjustable shelves. I make a hardwood template on the drill press, making a series of holes 1 in. apart. I use that template with a hand drill to cut the holes in the carcase.

Solid-wood details

To make the face frame, mill your stock to ¾ in. square and mark the pieces to length directly from the carcase. Cut the lap joints at the tablesaw, then glue and nail the face frame to the carcase. I use a nail gun for this, and later I fill the small nail holes with wood putty.

Next it's time to build the frame-and-panel back. After cutting the rails and stiles to size, cut their mortise-and-tenon joints (or dowel or biscuit joints if you're so inclined), and groove all the parts to accept the panels. Then dry-assemble the frame. Measure the

No-frills carcase. Becksvoort's native language may be solid wood, but he built the carcase of this utilitarian cabinet with plywood—dadoed, glued, and screwed.

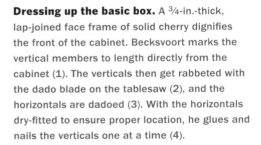

Dressing up the basic box. A ¾-in.-thick, lap-joined face frame of solid cherry dignifies the front of the cabinet. Becksvoort marks the vertical members to length directly from the cabinet (1). The verticals then get rabbeted with the dado blade on the tablesaw (2), and the horizontals are dadoed (3). With the horizontals dry-fitted to ensure proper location, he glues and nails the verticals one at a time (4).

Prepare to hang the drawers. With the drawer in place, transfer the location of the runner dado from the case to the drawer side. Becksvoort uses old credit cards as spacers beneath the drawer.

panel sizes directly from the frame, and cut the panels to fit. Assemble the back, and set it aside to cure. After the drawers are fitted, you'll glue and nail the assembly to the back of the carcase.

Smart storage areas

I made the side-hung drawers from solid wood, joining them with dovetails and then cutting grooves in the sides for the drawer runners. You could make the drawers from plywood if you wish, though the action of the runners will not be as smooth. At this point, install the runners inside the case and check the fit of the drawers. I like a drawer to be about $\frac{1}{16}$ in. narrower than the drawer pocket. Once the drawers are fitted, I mount the pulls. Flush pulls are preferable, since any protruding hardware may get in the way of clamping from above. I bought my pulls from Hamilton Marine; similar pulls are available from White Chapel.

Finally, make the mortise-and-tenoned frame-and-panel door. Fit it, install its pull, and hang it. Then apply your finish of choice to the cabinet and start putting all that stray stuff in its place.

Rout for the runners. Cut stopped grooves in the drawer sides to accept the solid-maple drawer runners. Becksvoort puts tape on the router table's fence to establish the location of the bit (top). Clean up the stopped end of the runner groove with a chisel (above).

Fix the runners. Becksvoort glues in the maple runners, using brads instead of clamps to hold them in place.

Beautify the back. With the drawer fitting finished, Becksvoort glues the solid cherry frame-and-panel back to the cabinet.

Fitting Flush-Mount Pulls

After roughing out a recess with a trim router to accept the main part of the pull, Becksvoort uses a countersink bit (below left) to create clearance for the screw dimples at the corners. Carbon paper and a gentle tap with a mallet (bottom left) mark the areas that need further excavation with a chisel (below right).

Minibench Works Wonders

STEVE LATTA

If necessity is the mother of invention, then my minibench is the proof. When I first built it, I wanted to raise my work to a more comfortable height, and to hold legs and other furniture parts for joinery cuts and detail work. Clamped on top of my regular bench, the minibench gets the work closer to my eyes without bending over. The 42-in.-long top is perfect for most furniture parts. It has a vise on one end, and the dog holes make it easy to hold parts. Plus there's plenty of clearance to use most types of clamps, making it easier to handplane and carve more accurately.

IN THE VISE

OR ON THE FRONT

CLAMP PARTS ON TOP

Get closer to the action. The minibench puts your work at a comfortable height for detail work. It's perfect for inlay, for trimming furniture parts, and for intricate carving.

Small but strong

Heavy-duty benchtop rests on I-beam-style legs for a sturdy, rack-free design

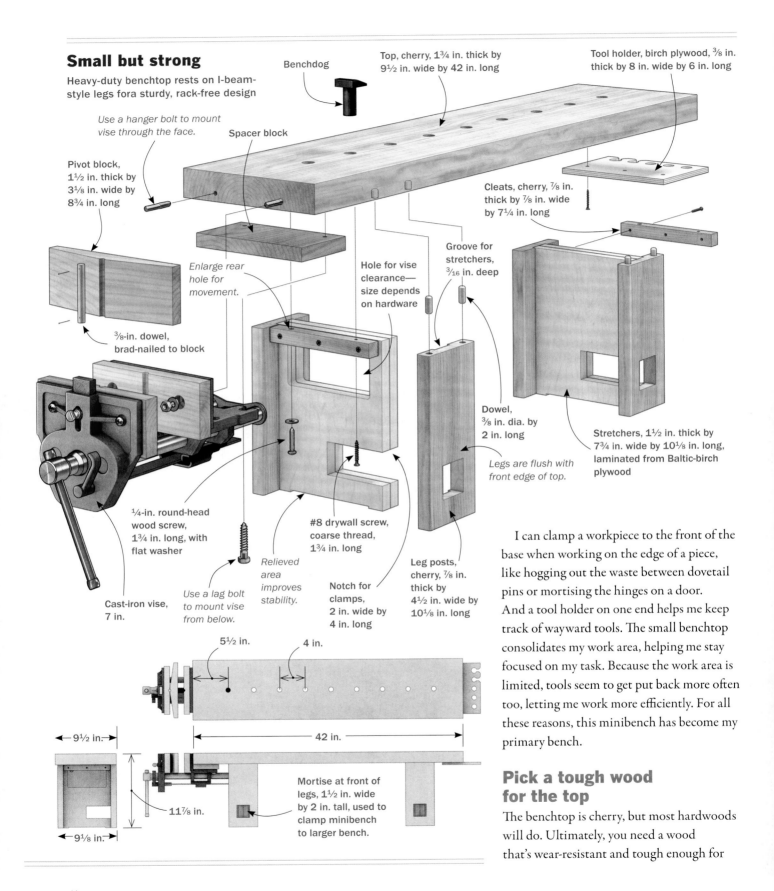

Benchdog

Top, cherry, 1¾ in. thick by 9½ in. wide by 42 in. long

Tool holder, birch plywood, ⅜ in. thick by 8 in. wide by 6 in. long

Use a hanger bolt to mount vise through the face.

Spacer block

Pivot block, 1½ in. thick by 3⅛ in. wide by 8¾ in. long

Enlarge rear hole for movement.

Hole for vise clearance— size depends on hardware

Groove for stretchers, ³⁄₁₆ in. deep

Cleats, cherry, ⅞ in. thick by ⅞ in. wide by 7¼ in. long

⅜-in. dowel, brad-nailed to block

Dowel, ⅜ in. dia. by 2 in. long

Legs are flush with front edge of top.

Stretchers, 1½ in. thick by 7¾ in. wide by 10⅛ in. long, laminated from Baltic-birch plywood

¼-in. round-head wood screw, 1¾ in. long, with flat washer

Relieved area improves stability.

#8 drywall screw, coarse thread, 1¾ in. long

Cast-iron vise, 7 in.

Use a lag bolt to mount vise from below.

Notch for clamps, 2 in. wide by 4 in. long

Leg posts, cherry, ⅞ in. thick by 4½ in. wide by 10⅛ in. long

5½ in.

4 in.

42 in.

9½ in.

11⅞ in.

9⅛ in.

Mortise at front of legs, 1½ in. wide by 2 in. tall, used to clamp minibench to larger bench.

I can clamp a workpiece to the front of the base when working on the edge of a piece, like hogging out the waste between dovetail pins or mortising the hinges on a door. And a tool holder on one end helps me keep track of wayward tools. The small benchtop consolidates my work area, helping me stay focused on my task. Because the work area is limited, tools seem to get put back more often too, letting me work more efficiently. For all these reasons, this minibench has become my primary bench.

Pick a tough wood for the top

The benchtop is cherry, but most hardwoods will do. Ultimately, you need a wood that's wear-resistant and tough enough for

Make the top

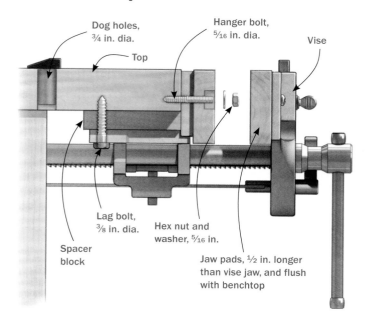

Dog holes, ¾ in. dia.

Hanger bolt, ⁵⁄₁₆ in. dia.

Top

Vise

Lag bolt, ⅜ in. dia.

Hex nut and washer, ⁵⁄₁₆ in.

Spacer block

Jaw pads, ½ in. longer than vise jaw, and flush with benchtop

Get the vise at the right height. Glue on a spacer block to locate the top of the vise ¹⁄₁₆ in. below the benchtop.

Drill the dog holes. To avoid blowout, Latta uses a spade bit in the drill press. He sets the depth stop for just after the point comes through, then flips the benchtop and finishes from the other side.

Bolt on the vise. Two hefty lag bolts and two hanger bolts help keep this vise right where it needs to be. With the benchtop upside down, set the vise in place and sink the lag bolts.

Take the bite out of the jaws. Bolt on hardwood pads to create a non-marring surface inside the vise jaws.

benchdogs and hold-downs. Mill the top to final dimensions, then drill the ¾-in.-dia. holes for the benchdogs at the drill press. They should be centered on the top and spaced about 4 in. apart down the length.

I wanted this compact bench to have a vise, so I chose an Eclipse 7-in. quick-release vise with a built-in benchdog—a must for holding long furniture parts like legs and rails. The quick-release makes for fast, easy adjustments. Mount the vise so that the jaws

Add a pivoting jaw for tapered work. A pivoting-jaw insert holds shaped furniture parts such as tapered legs in the vise. It's pretty simple to make. The pivoting block has a dowel attached to the back that rides in a matching half-round in the jaw pad, letting it swivel freely from side to side. The jaw is held in place by the vise's clamping pressure, so it's easy to remove. Not square? No problem. The pivoting block helps the vise conform to an out-of-square workpiece, putting pressure where needed.

Drill for the dowel. Clamp a backer block to the pivot block and drill a ⅜-in. hole on the seam to create a half-round channel for the dowel. Then drill the wooden jaw pads the same way.

Angle the back. Latta relieves the back on each side of the channel, so that the block can pivot freely in both directions.

Attach the dowel. Fasten the ⅜-in. dowel to the block with glue and a few small brads.

are ¹⁄₁₆ in. below the top of the bench, to protect you from dulling your sharp tools on the metal jaws. Set the height of the vise by using a spacer block mounted under the benchtop. The thickness of the block will depend on the vise you use. After gluing on the spacer block, you can install the vise.

I-beam legs are light and sturdy

The top rests on two strong I-beam legs, consisting of two hardwood posts and a stretcher made from a double thickness of ¾-in. Baltic-birch plywood. Both legs are mounted flush with the front edge of the top so that work can be clamped there. Each leg is mortised on the front to make it easy to clamp to your regular workbench. The leg closest to the vise needs a clearance hole for the vise hardware.

Glue up the stretchers for the legs and cut them to size. Relieve the bottom edge of the stretchers at the tablesaw using a dado blade and a miter gauge with a tall fence. This relieved area creates two small feet and helps keep the legs from rocking on any irregularities. Next, mark the front of the stretchers for the clamp notches. Make the two long cuts on the bandsaw using a fence and a piece of ¼-in. plywood underneath to prevent blowout, and finish the cut using a scrollsaw. Next, mark and cut out the mortise for the vise in one stretcher.

The leg posts are cut from one board. Mill it to thickness and width, then plow the groove for the stretchers. Use a stretcher to check the fit as you go. Now you can cut the posts to length.

Because sharp wood corners can break and chip easily during the normal wear and

Relieve the bottom of the stretcher. Latta uses a dado blade. He attaches a tall fence between two miter gauges and clamps on blocks to stop the cut 1 in. from each side.

Make the legs. The legs are shaped like an I-beam, with two hardwood posts connected by a thick plywood stretcher. A mortise in the front of each leg makes clamping to the benchtop quick and easy.

Cut out the mortises and notches. Drill the four corners of the mortise for the vise hardware and cut the sides on the scrollsaw. Make the long cuts for the notches on the bandsaw, then connect the ends on the scrollsaw.

Groove the leg post for the stretcher. Latta cuts the groove a little at a time, testing the fit with a stretcher as he goes.

Mark the leg post for the mortise. Use the stretcher to transfer the location of the clamp mortises onto the posts. Cut the mortises using a scrollsaw.

Pop in a pair of dowel centers.
Latta uses dowels to register the front of the benchtop flush with the legs. To locate the dowel holes in the top, he uses dowel centers.

Put some pressure on these points. A flat scrap of wood helps get the legs flush with the front of the benchtop. Then just add pressure. The pointed dowel centers will create a perfect set of dimples that mark where to drill.

tear of woodworking, ease the long edges of the posts with a ¼-in. roundover bit on the router table. Then use the stretchers to transfer the marks for the clamp mortises to the posts. Cut them out, drilling the corners on the drill press and cutting the sides with a scrollsaw. Glue and clamp the posts to the stretchers, making sure the top and bottom edges are flush.

The top is attached to the legs with dowels and screws. The screws go through a cleat attached to each leg stretcher. The dowels are located in the front post to keep the top flush with the legs. To accommodate wood movement and direct it toward the back of the bench, I enlarged the clearance holes for the rear screws that go through the cleat and into the top. To install the dowels, drill two holes in the top of each front leg post using a ⅜-in.-dia. brad-point bit. Then use dowel centers to transfer the location of these holes to the top. Put the centers in the holes, and with the top upside down, position the legs correctly and press down. Use the dimples made by the centers to drill the holes in the underside of the top. Insert the dowels into the holes without glue. Now screw the cleats to the legs, then screw the legs to the top.

The last step is to make the tool holder from a piece of ½-in. plywood and drill a few holes in it for chisels and screwdrivers. Notch a couple of holes to the edge—that will allow it to hold wide chisels—then screw it on and drop in your favorite tools. Now you have a serious work station, and it's time to get to work.

Cleats keep it all together.
Mount the cleats 1⁄32 in. shy of the top (above left), to ensure the legs are pulled tightly against the top. Put the legs in place, and screw them down. Sink the screws that connect each cleat to the top (left).

The Wired Workbench

JOHN WHITE

In a modern shop, a lot of work gets done with power tools such as routers, biscuit joiners, and random-orbit sanders. But most of us use them on benches designed around handplaning, which means everything from the height to the mass to the vises and benchdogs is geared toward hand-tool use. So the editors at *Fine Woodworking* decided to build a bench designed for power tools. They posted a blog on FineWoodworking.com, asking readers what they thought a "wired workbench" should be. A lot of great suggestions came in, and being a veteran of the *Fine Woodworking* shop and an inveterate inventor (see my "New-Fangled Workbench," *Fine Woodworking* #139), I was given the task of distilling readers' ideas into a user-friendly whole.

Power tools need electricity to run and they make dust by the fistful. So most people agreed that the first thing this bench needed was a built-in source of electricity and dust collection. I kept things simple by attaching a commercially available automated vacuum outlet, the iVAC switch box, that turns on the dust collection when you power up the tool. And I made room in the base for both a shop vacuum and an Oneida Dust Deputy, a min-iature cyclone that has proven its value trapping the fine dust (and all of the chips) before it gets to the vacuum and clogs the filter.

This wired workbench also is taller (38 in. total) than traditional benches, moving the tool and the workpiece up to a height where

Collect the dust, forget the fuss

Imagine locking down your workpieces quickly, and using your portable power tools without any dust or distractions.

CLEVER CLAMPING IS BUILT IN

Pipe clamps apply the pressure, and low-profile dogs stay out of the way of your tools.

SHOP VAC AT THE READY

Put a small vacuum in the cabinet and leave it there, ready to work. That way you won't forget to hook it up or be tempted to do without.

SMART VALET FOR CORDS AND HOSES

A simple hanger system manages these necessary evils, so they don't drag and disrupt your work.

HIGHER THAN A HAND-TOOL BENCH

Traditional benches are lower, so you can bear down on your bench planes. But power-tool tasks like routing and sanding are better at belly height.

DUST EMPTIES EASILY

The Dust Deputy grabs 99% of the chips and dust, dropping them into a box that's easy to empty and keeping the vacuum filter clean.

ONBOARD POWER

Plug your power tools into an automated vacuum switch that turns on the vacuum when you turn on the tool. It also runs the vacuum for a few seconds after the tool powers off.

you have better vision and control. It's wider, too, but not as long. I got rid of the traditional front and tail vises, opting for a simple but effective clamping system made from two pipe clamps. The benchdogs have soft heads that hold workpieces firmly, but won't dent or mar them. And there are locking casters underneath to make the bench mobile.

Finally, the wired workbench is much easier to make than a big, heavy traditional bench. Because it won't take the forces a hand-tool bench does, the entire bench is made from plywood. And there is no complicated joinery, just butt joints held together by screws. Where they show, I've used stainless-steel deck screws and finish washers for a clean, modern look.

If you already have a heavy hand-tool workbench, this one will make a great, mobile, secondary workstation. And if you rely mostly on power tools, this might be the only bench you need.

The base is a dust collector

It's not too difficult to cut accurate parts from plywood. (For a few tips, see one of my articles: "Best-Ever Outfeed Table," *Fine Woodworking* #202). I'll skip over that process now and just explain how the parts go together.

I put the vacuum and the mini-cyclone in the base for two reasons: First, enclosing the vacuum muffles it. Second, it makes the bench a self-contained unit. There's no vacuum trailing behind it like a baby elephant behind its mother.

Start assembling the base with the bottom panel, pre-drilling holes for the casters. Then attach the front panel to the bottom. Screw the interior divider to the base and then to the front panel. Next, attach the back panel to the base and divider, but before you do, drill the ventilation hole (the power cord for the iVac switch also passes through this hole).

An apron runs across the top of the door opening at both ends of the base. Each apron is screwed to plywood cleats. The top cleat attaches the top assembly. The side cleats serve as door stops. After assembling the aprons and cleats, screw them between the front and back panels.

Then turn over the base and bolt the casters to it. Flip the cabinet back over and install the doors. Attach the lower door stops to the sides of the cabinet and to the bottom panel. Then screw the pivoting door "locks" to the apron.

Collect the dust in an airtight box. The Dust Deputy is a plastic cyclone typically attached to the lid of a 5-gallon bucket, which collects the chips and dust when they fall out of the cyclone. But such an assembly is too tall to fit inside the base cabinet, so I came up with another way to collect the debris. Of course, that meant overcoming a big challenge, because for the cyclone to work properly, the box needs to be airtight. Fortunately, I found an easy way to do that, because—and this is the cool part—you don't need any special tools or materials to make it.

The cyclone sits on top of a box, and inside the box is a removable drawer that catches the dust and chips. When it is full, you just open the box, pull out the drawer, dump it in a trash can, and put it back in.

The butt joints in the box are tight enough to prevent airflow and the door can be used to create a tight seal around the opening. Just apply foam gasket—the kind used for weather stripping on entry doors—around the opening for the door, mitering the corners and gluing them together using cyanoacrylate glue. When the door closes against the gasket, it creates an airtight seal.

To fine-tune how much the door compresses the gasket, I drove two drywall screws into the back of the outer dust bin. Adjusting the screws in and out moves the box farther

Build the base first

Rather than fill the interior with drawers, we designed it to hide and muffle a shop vacuum and hold a dust separator. Construction is simple and solid: ¾-in. plywood and drywall screws.

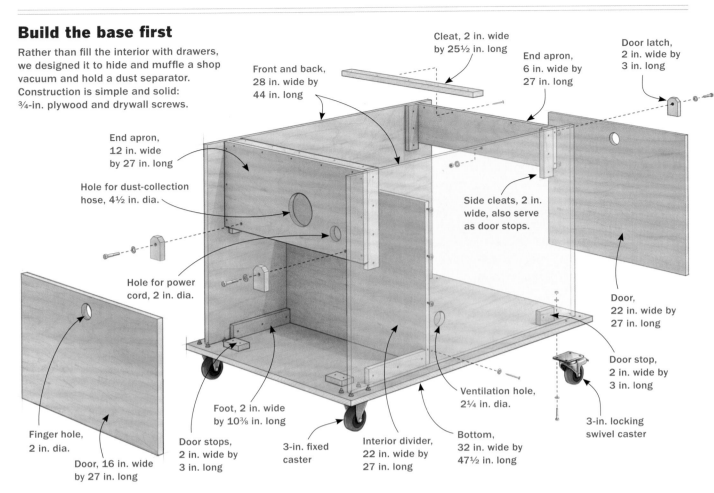

Cleat, 2 in. wide by 25½ in. long

End apron, 6 in. wide by 27 in. long

Door latch, 2 in. wide by 3 in. long

Front and back, 28 in. wide by 44 in. long

End apron, 12 in. wide by 27 in. long

Hole for dust-collection hose, 4½ in. dia.

Side cleats, 2 in. wide, also serve as door stops.

Hole for power cord, 2 in. dia.

Door, 22 in. wide by 27 in. long

Finger hole, 2 in. dia.

Door, 16 in. wide by 27 in. long

Foot, 2 in. wide by 10⅜ in. long

Door stops, 2 in. wide by 3 in. long

3-in. fixed caster

Interior divider, 22 in. wide by 27 in. long

Ventilation hole, 2¼ in. dia.

Bottom, 32 in. wide by 47½ in. long

Door stop, 2 in. wide by 3 in. long

3-in. locking swivel caster

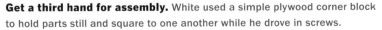

Get a third hand for assembly. White used a simple plywood corner block to hold parts still and square to one another while he drove in screws.

END APRON HOLE LOCATIONS

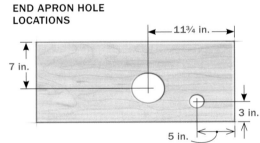

11¾ in.

7 in.

3 in.

5 in.

Add aprons for stiffness. Screw through the face into the cleats. On the cyclone end, pre-drill holes for the vacuum hose and power cords with a circle cutter.

Mini-cyclone drops dust into a bin

A mini-cyclone separates chips and dust out of the vacuum's airflow, dropping them into an easy-to-empty dust bin below.

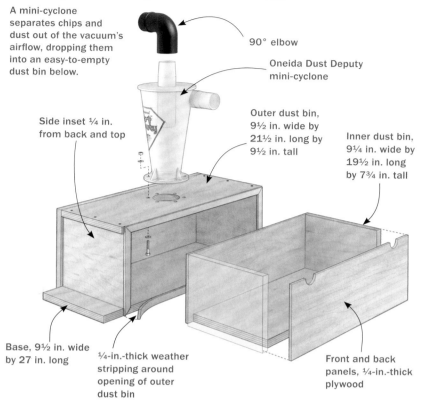

90° elbow

Oneida Dust Deputy mini-cyclone

Side inset ¼ in. from back and top

Outer dust bin, 9½ in. wide by 21½ in. long by 9½ in. tall

Inner dust bin, 9¼ in. wide by 19½ in. long by 7¾ in. tall

Base, 9½ in. wide by 27 in. long

¼-in.-thick weather stripping around opening of outer dust bin

Front and back panels, ¼-in.-thick plywood

Fine-tune the air seal

A door on the cabinet presses tightly against weather stripping on the dust bin, so the inner bin can be loose. Stops at the bottom and latches at the top of the door create even pressure. Use drywall screws on the back of the dust bin to push it back and forth to fine-tune how much the weather stripping is compressed by the door.

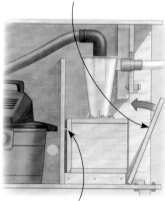

Use drywall screws on the back of the dust bin to push it back and forth to fine-tune how much the weather stripping is compressed by the door.

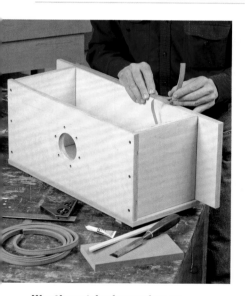

Weather stripping makes an airtight seal. Miter the corners with a chisel after you apply the stripping, and glue the corners together with cyanoacrylate glue.

Put the Deputy on the case. To create an airtight seal, apply a bead of acrylic caulk to the mini-cyclone's flange before putting it on the bin.

Connect the vacuum to the mini-cyclone. A 90° elbow makes the tight turn under the bench's top without restricting airflow like a crimped hose would.

Layered top has room for clamps

This plywood top assembly has a clamping system built into it. The layered construction makes it easy to create tongued channels for the sliding benchdog blocks and a cavity for the pipe clamps.

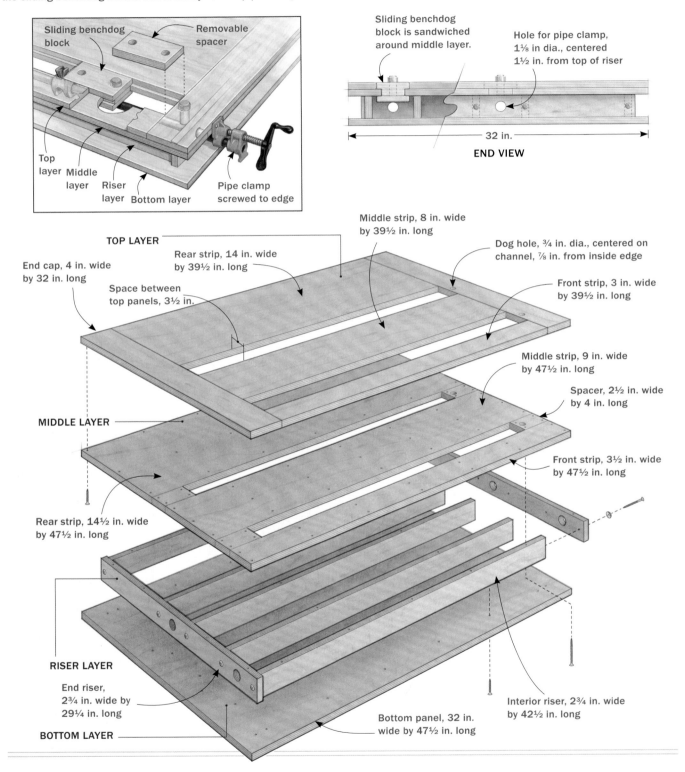

Sliding benchdog block

Removable spacer

Top layer

Middle layer

Riser layer

Bottom layer

Pipe clamp screwed to edge

Sliding benchdog block is sandwiched around middle layer.

Hole for pipe clamp, 1⅛ in. dia., centered 1½ in. from top of riser

32 in.

END VIEW

TOP LAYER

End cap, 4 in. wide by 32 in. long

Space between top panels, 3½ in.

Rear strip, 14 in. wide by 39½ in. long

Middle strip, 8 in. wide by 39½ in. long

Dog hole, ¾ in. dia., centered on channel, ⅞ in. from inside edge

Front strip, 3 in. wide by 39½ in. long

Middle strip, 9 in. wide by 47½ in. long

Spacer, 2½ in. wide by 4 in. long

MIDDLE LAYER

Rear strip, 14½ in. wide by 47½ in. long

Front strip, 3½ in. wide by 47½ in. long

RISER LAYER

End riser, 2¾ in. wide by 29¼ in. long

Interior riser, 2¾ in. wide by 42½ in. long

Bottom panel, 32 in. wide by 47½ in. long

BOTTOM LAYER

Build the top two layers first. To connect the top and middle layers pre-drill and countersink for the screws and use an offcut from the plywood to keep the edges aligned as you drive the screws.

Use spacers to locate slots for clamps. Make sure they're dimensioned and placed accurately, because they determine where you drill holes for the stationary benchdogs.

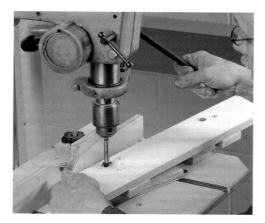

Drill for the stationary benchdogs. Leave the spacers attached and drill through both pieces at once. Use scraps to support the far end of the assembly.

from and closer to the door and compresses the gasket less or more.

Finally, to complete the airtight box, apply a bead of acrylic caulk around the opening for the cyclone before bolting it in place.

The top is a vise

The cool thing about this top is that, like my new-fangled workbench, it has a clamping system built into it. All you need are two ¾-in. pipe clamps—this bench is designed for Jorgensen No. 50 Pony clamps—some ¾-in.-dia. dowel, and ¾-in.-internal-dia. vinyl tubing. The dowel is cut into short lengths to make benchdogs and the tubing slides over the dogs to keep them from marring or denting your work, something you don't want to have happen when you're sanding a door just before applying a finish.

Here's how it works. A block of plywood with a dog hole drilled in it is pushed against the sliding jaw of the pipe clamp. The other jaw is fixed to the apron. You can move the sliding jaw wherever you need it, and the dog hole moves along with it.

The top is made from layers of plywood strips, but it is plenty rigid for power-tool work (and some hand-tool work like light planing). Screw the top and middle layers together. Mark the locations of the stationary

benchdogs, partially disassemble the parts, and drill the holes.

Now that the basic structure of the top has been assembled, make and attach the riser layer. The two end risers need holes for the pipes to pass through. Drill them at the drill press.

Next, make and install the sliding bench-dog blocks. Assemble the layers and drill a hole for the benchdog. Take off the bottom layer, add some tape to make the groove a bit

Add the riser frame and sliding dogs. Use long screws to screw down through the frame pieces and into the top.

Make the sliding benchdog blocks. After drilling dog holes through the assembled blocks, take off the bottom layer and put the blocks in place. Three stacked pieces of blue tape, added after the dog holes are drilled, create enough play for the block to slide easily (use a knife to cut openings in the tape).

Sliding benchdog blocks

Top, ¾ in. thick by 3½ in. wide by 6 in. long

Middle, ¾ in. thick by 2½ in. wide by 6 in. long

Put tape between bottom and middle layers.

Dog hole, ¾ in. dia.

Secure the sliding benchdogs with screws from the bottom.

Bottom, ½ in. thick

Install the low-cost clamping system. Whether you're sanding or routing, the workpiece needs to be held still. White's ingenious "vise" is nothing more than ¾-in. pipe clamps and a clever system of sliding blocks and dogs, but it gets the job done and applies pressure close to the bench's surface—without sticking up and getting in the way. To start put the top on the base. It's heavier than it looks, but one person can do it. Screw through the cleats in the base, into the top.

Install the pipe clamps. Put the bare end in and through the adjustable clamp head. Tighten it completely, and mark it where it's flush with the top's edge. Take it out, cut it to length, and put it back. Screw the fixed head to the bench through pre-drilled holes (inset), so you can open and close it without holding the head.

Low-tech benchdogs. A sharp knife is all you need to cut the plastic tubing that fits over the dowels (above) so they won't mar or dent workpieces. Use filler blocks to cover the slot (right). You need several of different lengths for complete coverage no matter where the benchdog block and clamp head are.

Tame hoses and cords from above

Nothing is more annoying than a cord or hose that continually catches and drags as you try to control a tool. White solved that problem with an overhead rack for both.

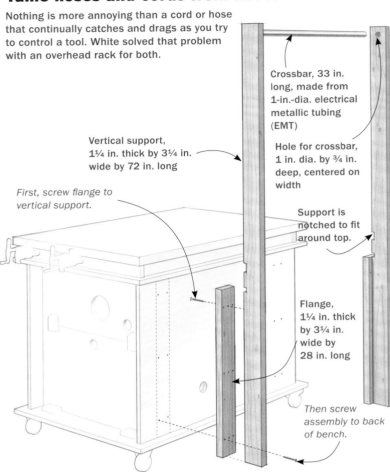

Vertical support, 1¼ in. thick by 3¼ in. wide by 72 in. long

Crossbar, 33 in. long, made from 1-in.-dia. electrical metallic tubing (EMT)

Hole for crossbar, 1 in. dia. by ¾ in. deep, centered on width

First, screw flange to vertical support.

Support is notched to fit around top.

Flange, 1¼ in. thick by 3¼ in. wide by 28 in. long

Then screw assembly to back of bench.

Elegantly simple. White used a key ring and O-ring bought at a local hardware store to suspend the hose. Another one holds the cord. They slide easily over the electrical tubing used for the crossbar.

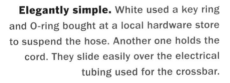

wider than the tongue on the top, and install the blocks. Now attach the bottom panel to the risers. Then set the entire assembly onto the base and attach it by screwing through the cleats and into the bottom panel.

Make filler blocks for the slots. Then make some benchdogs from a length of dowel and slip some vinyl tubing over one end. Finally, install the pipe clamps.

A Saw Bench Is a Versatile Addition to Your Shop

MEGAN FITZPATRICK

A saw bench is not simply a low sawhorse; it's a completely different animal. A pair of benches makes the use of panel saws and full-size handsaws efficient and comfortable when crosscutting and ripping boards. I also use them for drilling, finishing, helping brace workpieces, sitting and standing on, and much more.

I'll show you how to build one saw bench using hand tools and home center material, but for many operations, two—and sometimes a small herd—of saw benches are required. When I make multiples I prep the stock at the same time (at least the parts I use machinery to prep), but I build them separately. There aren't any tricky setups to replicate, so I don't see an advantage to building them simultaneously.

These benches are built to fit the maker. After you have your saw bench together, you'll trim the legs to make the top of the bench hit just below your kneecap. I'm just shy of 5 ft., 6 in.; my saw bench is 17½ in. high. If you're remarkably tall (more than about 6 ft., 5 in.), make your bench legs' rough length a little longer than shown in the drawing; if you're petite, you might want to raise the height of the braces so they remain a bit above the floor when you trim the legs to length.

How to use it

RIPPING

With one knee on top of the board to keep it in place (p. 129), begin the ripcut on the end overhanging the front of the bench. As you approach the V-notch in the top, shift the work forward to continue ripping. For longer boards, use two benches to support the work. To maintain support of the entire workpiece later in the cut, shift it back and continue cutting between the benches. If the workpiece is wide enough, saw to the side of the bench.

CROSSCUTTING

The foot of your dominant leg should be on the floor with the board butted against the top of your shin (left). Keep your other knee atop the work to hold it. As you approach the end of the cut, reach around with your free hand to grasp the offcut so that it doesn't break off.

WORK SUPPORT

A saw bench makes an excellent surface for finishing (especially large pieces, (right). You can also clamp work to a saw bench for boring or mortising; the low height makes it possible to get your body right over the work.

Find, cut, and prep your stock

At your local home center, pick through the 2x6 white pine to find the straightest, clearest 10-ft. board available.

Typically, I recommend cutting each part as you need it, referencing off your work. However, this project is a rare instance in which you should mark out and cut all the pieces to match the cut list before starting the joinery. That's because no one part relies on another for its finished size, and because you need the parts cut and ready for direct transfer of measurements for the joints.

Leg joinery

Flatten the least attractive side of each leg with a jointer plane, then mark it as the true face. Now plane the edges, using a square to check that they are perfectly square to the true face, and shoot the top ends to ensure that they, too, are square to the true face. The show face can be cleaned up later if you wish. All the joinery layout will be on the true face and on the square end and edges; the show face of the legs doesn't affect the joinery.

The legs get angled half laps that fit into notches in the top. To lay out the half laps, set a marking gauge to ½ in. and scribe a line off the true face onto the top of each leg. Now set the gauge to 1½ in., and scribe the shoulder line on each leg, registering off the top.

Both the cheeks and shoulders are angled at 10°. Set a bevel gauge to 10° and use a pencil to mark the angles. Now saw the cheeks. Use a chisel, bevel toward the waste, to make a small V-shaped notch on the corner. Set a fine-toothed ripsaw into the notch, then saw down your layout line.

Saw bench

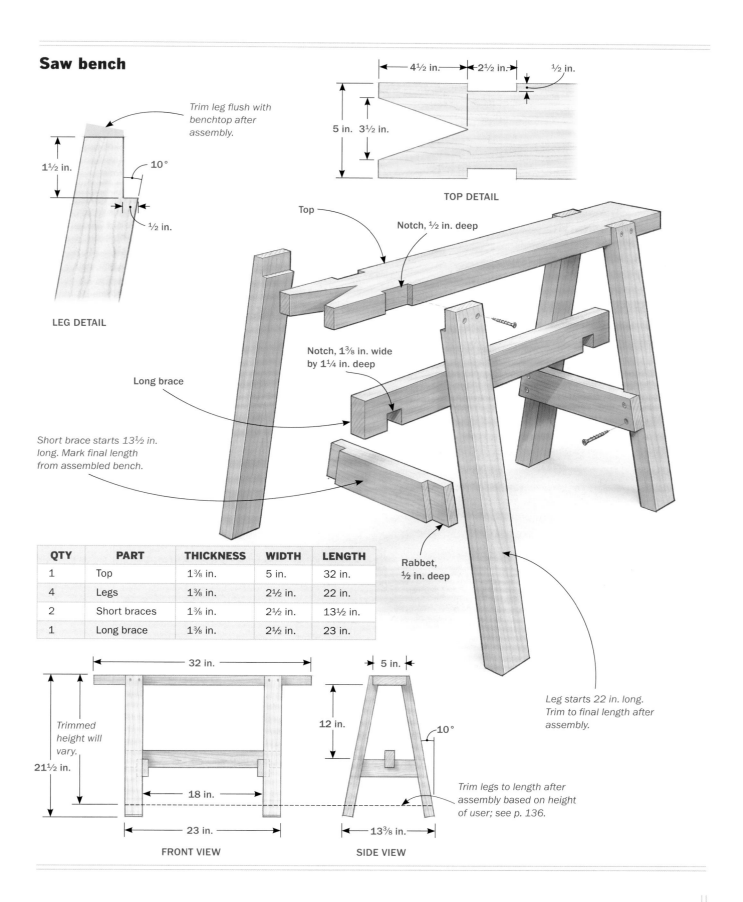

LEG DETAIL

1½ in.

10°

½ in.

Trim leg flush with benchtop after assembly.

TOP DETAIL

4½ in.

2½ in.

½ in.

5 in.

3½ in.

Top

Notch, ½ in. deep

Notch, 1⅜ in. wide by 1¼ in. deep

Long brace

Short brace starts 13½ in. long. Mark final length from assembled bench.

Rabbet, ½ in. deep

Leg starts 22 in. long. Trim to final length after assembly.

QTY	PART	THICKNESS	WIDTH	LENGTH
1	Top	1⅜ in.	5 in.	32 in.
4	Legs	1⅜ in.	2½ in.	22 in.
2	Short braces	1⅜ in.	2½ in.	13½ in.
1	Long brace	1⅜ in.	2½ in.	23 in.

32 in.

Trimmed height will vary.

21½ in.

18 in.

23 in.

FRONT VIEW

5 in.

12 in.

10°

13⅜ in.

SIDE VIEW

Trim legs to length after assembly based on height of user; see p. 136.

A SAW BENCH IS A VERSATILE ADDITION TO YOUR SHOP | **131**

Notch the legs. An angled half lap in the legs creates the splay when the legs are attached to the top. With a bevel gauge set to 10°, mark a line to establish the cheek. With the gauge still set to 10°, mark a line to establish the shoulder.

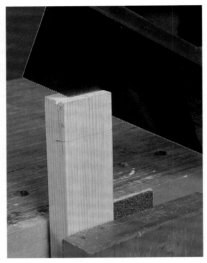

Cut the cheek. Cut a shallow kerf into the end grain, then tilt the tenon saw to follow the vertical cheek line. This will help you to follow the two lines accurately as you saw.

Cut the shoulder. Deepen the shoulder line slightly with a chisel. This small trench helps to position the saw when starting the cut.

Next, cut the shoulders. Drop a chisel into your marking gauge line and cut a small V-shaped trench along the joint line. Secure the leg against a bench hook on your bench, then use the trench to guide a fine crosscut saw as you saw down to the cheek. Save the offcuts to use later as clamping cauls, and clean up the cheeks.

Top joinery

Just as with the legs, with the top the true face is the side that won't show. So true up the less attractive face, mark it as true, then square the long edges to that face.

Next, lay out the V-shaped ripping notch on both faces at the front end of the top. Use a pencil to mark a centerline, then measure 5 in. from the front edge and make a tick mark. Measure and mark ¾ in. from both edges at the end. Connect the dots with a straightedge. Use a ripsaw or crosscut saw to cut the notch, then clean up the cuts with a rasp as necessary.

Now lay out and cut the notches for the legs. On both long edges, measure 4½ in. from each end, then register a marking knife against a square to knife in the outside shoulder of each notch. Use the leg to locate the other shoulder of the notch. Use a cutting gauge to lay out the notch bottoms, ½ in. from the edge. Saw the shoulders of each notch, then remove most of the waste with a coping saw, or pop it out with a chisel. Use a large router plane to clean up the bottoms.

Remember those offcuts you saved? Tape them to the top of the legs, narrow side

Clean up the joint. With the leg in a hand-screw clamp, align the cheek flush to the top of the jaws. Then use the jaws to guide a wide chisel as you clean up the cheek cuts. Because the cheek and shoulder are at a 90° angle, you can use a shoulder plane to clean up the inside corner.

Shape the top. Use a panel saw or full-size handsaw to cut the V of the ripping notch. Because the cuts are at an angle, either a crosscut or rip saw will work.

Mark the leg notches. Align the leg to a knifed line 4½ in. from the end of the top, then scribe along the other side of the leg with a knife. Finish by marking the depth of the notch on each face of the top.

Cut the notches. Use a crosscut saw to cut both shoulders of the notch. Use a coping saw and chisel to remove the waste. Then use a router plane to clean up the bottom, working into the center from each face so as not to blow out the back.

down. Brush glue in the notches and on the cheeks of the legs, then clamp the legs in place, making sure the top is firmly seated on the shoulders. Thanks to those offcuts, the clamps should close squarely. Because the assembly is upside down, you can leave it in clamps and move on to the next few steps while the glue dries.

Add the short braces

The two short braces get lapped onto the inside of the legs, but the legs don't get a corresponding notch. True up the two short braces, and mark the true face (this time, it is the show face). The top edge of each short brace is located 12 in. from the underside of the top, so cut a 12-in. spacer block from

Glue the legs to the top. Use the tapered offcuts from the leg half-laps as clamping cauls. Clamp the assembly upside down with the top shimmed up so the clamps will apply pressure to the center of the joint.

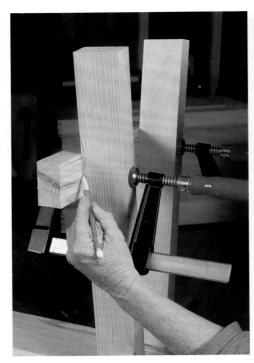

Mark the short and long braces. With the short braces clamped in place, mark the inside edge with a knife. Use a pencil to mark the outside edges. Saw them to length, then cut the half-laps. Glue and clamp them in place, and mark and cut the notches in the long brace. Then glue that in place.

scrap, and use that to position each brace on the inside of the legs, with the true face against the legs. Clamp the braces to the legs, and mark the braces for length with a pencil.

Register a knife against the inside face of the legs to mark out the shoulders on the braces. After unclamping and crosscutting the braces to length, set a cutting gauge to ½ in. and mark the cheeks. Cut the cheeks and shoulders, then clean up the cheeks with a router plane and the shoulders with a shoulder plane. Glue the short braces to the legs, and clamp them in place while you cut the joinery for the long brace.

Long brace joinery

On the long brace, the true surface is not a face, but the bottom edge. So true up the least-attractive edge, then true both faces 90° to that edge.

Center the long brace end-to-end, then clamp it in position on the short braces. Use a marking knife to scribe the location of the short braces on the true edge of the long brace. Then remove the long brace to lay out the notches that join it to the short braces. Remove most of the waste with a coping saw or chisel; clean up the bottoms with a router plane.

If you want to be fancy, plane chamfers on the top edge of the long brace, cut ogees on the end, or whatever you choose. You can also do nothing here.

Nail, clean, and level

Nail in the same order that you glued and clamped; legs to top first, short braces to legs, and finally long brace to short braces. Then, use a flush-cutting saw to trim the legs flush to the top.

Now measure from the floor to the bottom of your kneecap and note that number. Shim the saw bench level on a flat

Drill for the nails. Without pilot holes, the wedge shape of cut nails or square-shanked nails could split the work. Fitzpatrick uses diamond-head forged nails from Clouterie Rivierre, available from leevalley.com or directly at forgednails.com.

Flush the legs to the top. A cheap pull saw works great as a flush-cutting saw on large work. Just be sure to take it to your sharpening stones to remove the set from both sides before using it for this purpose.

The right height for you. Measure from the floor to the bottom of your kneecap. Level the saw bench on a flat surface, shimming the legs as necessary. Use a scrap and half-pencil to mark around all four sides of each leg, then cut them to length.

surface, then measure down from the top of the bench to the level surface. Subtract your leg-measurement number from the current saw bench height number, and cut a scrap the length of the result. Use a scrap and a pencil to mark each leg.

You don't need a finish on the saw bench. It will acquire its own with age and while finishing other projects.

Now go build that second saw bench.

6 Essential Bench Jigs

MICHAEL PEKOVICH

When starting out with hand tools, it doesn't take long to realize that the cutting force of the tool tends to move the workpiece in the direction of the cut. One of the secrets to hand-tool success is stopping that movement.

While clamping a piece in a vise or to the benchtop can work, often it's overkill. Not

only that, but clamping and unclamping adds a lot of time to the process. A better method is to use a planing stop or saw hook, which take advantage of the cutting force of the tool to keep the workpiece in place.

When handplaning, the tool drives the workpiece forward. If you add a stop at the front edge of the board, you can plane all

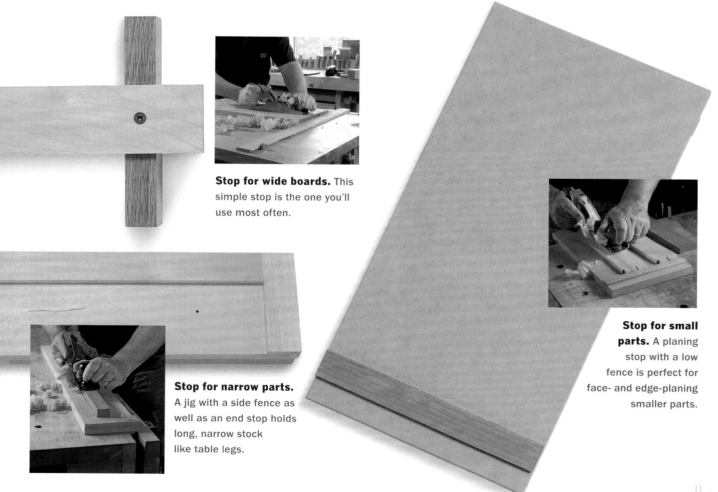

Stop for wide boards. This simple stop is the one you'll use most often.

Stop for narrow parts. A jig with a side fence as well as an end stop holds long, narrow stock like table legs.

Stop for small parts. A planing stop with a low fence is perfect for face- and edge-planing smaller parts.

Shooting board for end grain. This is an indispensable jig for squaring crosscuts and truing miters.

Saw hook for crosscuts and miters. With a tall, kerfed fence, this saw hook makes quick work of crosscuts and miters.

Saw block for thin stock. To cut small, thin stock to length, a saw block clamped in a vise is a better choice than the full-size saw hook.

day without the piece moving. In addition, it's fast and easy to flip the stock to surface the other faces without messing around with clamps or vises.

A saw hook works the same way. Hold the workpiece against the saw hook's fence, and you'll get faster, more accurate cuts every time.

Planing stops and saw hooks can take many forms. Some have a cleat that rests against the

edge of the bench to keep the jig in place, while others are clamped in place.

I use one of these bench jigs just about any time I pick up a handplane or saw. Here I'll cover the ones I use most often. Some take just minutes to make while others are a little more involved. Even so, you can knock all of them out in an afternoon, and then get back to serious work.

T-stop handles most of your planing tasks

The T-stop is the easiest to make and the one I use most often. In its simplest form, it consists of a thin fence screwed to a cleat that gets clamped in a vise. The fence can be as long as your bench is wide. The cleat should be thick enough to accept the screw. Anything ¾ in. or more is fine. When attaching the fence, make sure that the screw head is recessed below the surface to avoid contact with the plane blade.

To use the stop, clamp the cleat in a vise and then secure the opposite end—you can clamp it to the far side of the benchtop, or drill a dog hole opposite the vise and drop in a benchdog. The single screw allows the fence to pivot until it hits the benchdog, so the cleat placement in the vise doesn't have to be right on. With the stop in place, you can tackle boards and panels as wide as your benchtop. You can also edge-plane stock up to 6 in. wide by standing it on edge against the stop.

Two scraps and a screw are all you need. The T-square jig consists of a long fence attached to a cleat with a recessed screw. To use it, clamp the cleat in your vise and secure the opposite end with a clamp or benchdog (below).

T-Stop for wide boards

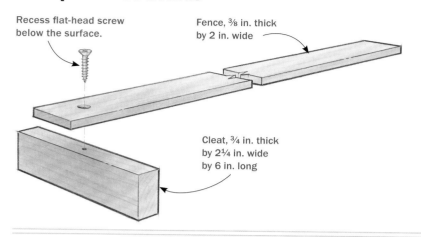

Recess flat-head screw below the surface.

Fence, ⅜ in. thick by 2 in. wide

Cleat, ¾ in. thick by 2¼ in. wide by 6 in. long

Plane away. The long, low fence offers support all the way across the benchtop without the need to clamp parts in place. Use it to face-plane larger parts and panels (above). In addition, you can edge-plane parts up to 6 in. wide (right).

Get a grip on legs and other thin parts

To plane long, narrow parts, which have a tendency to pivot, I use a stop that provides lateral support as well. Attach two thin strips to a plywood base at right angles and add a cleat on the bottom so it can be clamped in the vise. The stop keeps the work from pivoting, even when you skew the plane for a smoother cut. When chamfering or shaping legs, add V-blocks to the stop to support the stock at 45°.

Stop for narrow parts

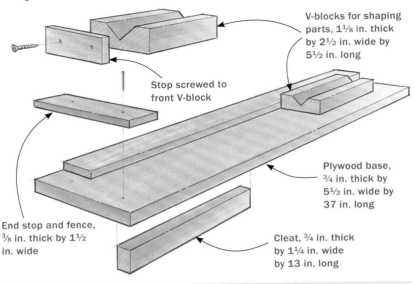

V-blocks for shaping parts, 1⅛ in. thick by 2½ in. wide by 5½ in. long

Stop screwed to front V-block

Plywood base, ¾ in. thick by 5½ in. wide by 37 in. long

End stop and fence, ⅜ in. thick by 1½ in. wide

Cleat, ¾ in. thick by 1¼ in. wide by 13 in. long

Easy to build, easy to use. Pekovich glues and pins the thin end stop and fence to the plywood base (above). He also glues a cleat to the bottom of the jig, which allows it to be clamped in place (right). The fence prevents long parts like table legs from pivoting during planing (far right).

V-blocks support stock at an angle. For shaping or chamfering long, narrow parts, screw a pair of beveled blocks to each end of the jig (above). The front block has an end stop screwed to the face to hold the stock in place while shaping (right).

Shooting board for squaring end cuts

I depend on this shooting board to square up the ends of parts perfectly. In the past, I've tried to attach a fixed fence at exactly 90°, but I've always needed to shim it square later. On this version, though, I made the fence adjustable so that I can square it up as needed.

The heart of the jig is the plywood base, which has two layers glued together to create a bed for the plane. The subbase is dadoed to receive a cleat that registers against the edge of my bench. The top layer has a groove along the top edge to guide a speed square that I use while shooting miters. The hardwood fence pivots on a steel pin, and it has a knob on the opposite end to lock in the setting. Drill the clearance hole for the knob's threaded shaft slightly oversize to allow some adjustment.

Because there's just a small range of adjustment, the fence holes need to be drilled so that the fence is roughly square to begin with. To do this, pre-drill the fence and clamp it in place as square as you can with its end just overhanging the step in the base. Then use the fence as a guide as you drill into the base. Drive the steel pin into the smaller hole in the base, and thread an insert into the larger hole. Once the fence is

Shooting board for end cuts

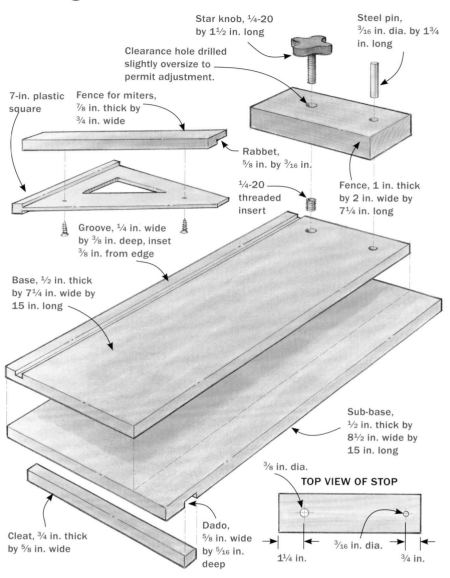

Star knob, ¼-20 by 1½ in. long

Steel pin, ³⁄₁₆ in. dia. by 1¾ in. long

Clearance hole drilled slightly oversize to permit adjustment.

7-in. plastic square

Fence for miters, ⁷⁄₈ in. thick by ¾ in. wide

Rabbet, ⁵⁄₈ in. by ³⁄₁₆ in.

¼-20 threaded insert

Fence, 1 in. thick by 2 in. wide by 7¼ in. long

Groove, ¼ in. wide by ³⁄₈ in. deep, inset ³⁄₈ in. from edge

Base, ½ in. thick by 7¼ in. wide by 15 in. long

Sub-base, ½ in. thick by 8½ in. wide by 15 in. long

³⁄₈ in. dia.

TOP VIEW OF STOP

³⁄₁₆ in. dia.

1¼ in.

¾ in.

Cleat, ¾ in. thick by ⁵⁄₈ in. wide

Dado, ⁵⁄₈ in. wide by ⁵⁄₁₆ in. deep

TIP Drilling for the fence. Because the oversize hole only allows for slight adjustment, the fence holes in the base should be drilled as accurately as possible. To make this easier, pre-drill the fence, clamp it square to the jig with its end extending slightly from the edge of the jig, and use it as a guide for drilling. Tap the pin into the small hole and thread an insert into the larger hole.

Squaring up is easy. To set up for shooting, loosen the adjustment knob and square the fence to the edge of the jig with a combination square. The first few passes with the plane will flush the fence to the edge of the jig, creating a zero-clearance back stop for planing parts.

Dos and Don'ts of using a shooting board

PUSH DOWN AGAINST THE BASE, NOT INTO THE FENCE

The reference face for the plane is its side, so to maintain a square cut and avoid paring into the fence, exert pressure downward.

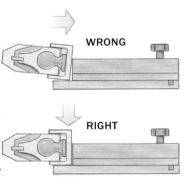

WRONG

RIGHT

KEEP THE WORK-PIECE FLUSH TO THE EDGE

Overhanging the workpiece will result in an angled cut and tearout along the back edge. Instead, set the plane in place and slide the workpiece against the sole ahead of the blade, and then make the cut.

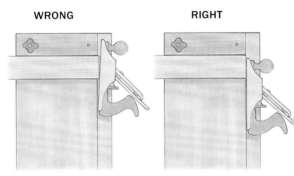

WRONG

RIGHT

Speed square makes for accurate miters. Adapting a Methods of Work tip from Sean Montague, Pekovich uses a plastic square with a hardwood fence to shoot mitered ends of parts. The base of the square slides in a groove in the base and registers against the fence.

in place, plane its end flush with the step in the base to create a zero-clearance backstop for planing.

When working end grain I use a low-angle smoothing plane on its side. It rides on the bed and registers against the edge of the base. Place the plane on the bed and snug it up to the edge. Then place the workpiece against the fence and slide it until it contacts the plane sole ahead of the blade. Set the plane for a light cut so that it doesn't get bogged down in the end grain.

For shooting miters I use a speed square with a wood fence attached to it. You need to trim a corner of the square, so buy a plastic one. The base of the square rides in the groove, and you can dial in the miter angle by adjusting the shooting-board fence.

Stop for planing small parts

This stop gets quite a bit of use in my shop. It consists of an MDF base with dadoes for a fence and cleat. The dadoes might seem like overkill, but they ensure that the cleat and stop are square to the edge. More important, this design makes it easy to glue the fence in place, so there aren't any screws to nick my plane iron. Also, I typically make more than one stop at a time, so setting up the dado blade is worth the effort. The fence is only $\frac{3}{16}$ in. high, which allows me to easily plane stock down to $\frac{1}{4}$ in. thick.

The other advantage of the jig is the ability to edge-plane small parts. Just lay the workpiece flat and slide it over until its edge extends beyond the jig. Then place your plane on its side against the bench to plane the edge. This is a great way to ensure a square edge on thin parts.

Dadoes simplify assembly. The fence and cleat on this jig, as well as those on the saw hook (p. 144), are glued into shallow dadoes in the bases. This ensures a sturdy, square glue-up of the jig parts.

Stop for small parts

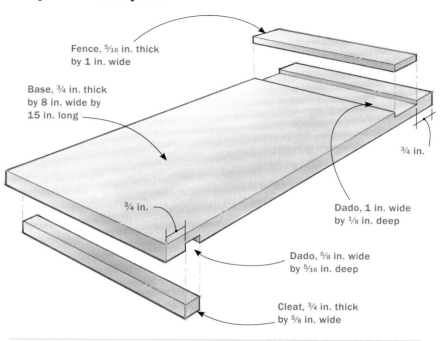

Fence, $\frac{5}{16}$ in. thick by 1 in. wide

Base, $\frac{3}{4}$ in. thick by 8 in. wide by 15 in. long

$\frac{3}{4}$ in.

$\frac{3}{4}$ in.

Dado, 1 in. wide by $\frac{1}{8}$ in. deep

Dado, $\frac{5}{8}$ in. wide by $\frac{5}{16}$ in. deep

Cleat, $\frac{3}{4}$ in. thick by $\frac{5}{8}$ in. wide

A low fence for thin parts. Because small parts also tend to be thin, the fence only protrudes $\frac{3}{16}$ in. above the deck (above left). It can be difficult to maintain a square edge while planing thin stock, so Pekovich lays the part and plane on their sides to make edge-planing easier (above).

Saw hook for crosscuts and miters

I use a saw hook to tackle sawing at the benchtop. It has a cleat and a fence with slots for the saw at 45° and 90° angles. In the past I've simply sawn through the fence to create the slots, but it's difficult to make a plumb cut at the exact angle. To make it easier, start by running a shallow dado for the fence. Then precut the fence into blocks at the chopsaw and reassemble them as you glue them into the dado. Use a card scraper to space the blocks. The resulting slot is slightly wider than the sawkerf, which prevents the saw from binding during a cut.

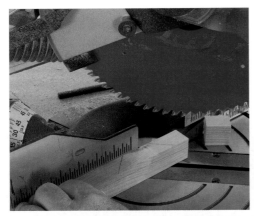

Chop and assemble the fence parts. Cut the fence apart at the chopsaw and glue the parts into the dado in the base. Pekovich uses a card scraper to space the parts and create a slot for the saw.

Saw hook for crosscuts and miters

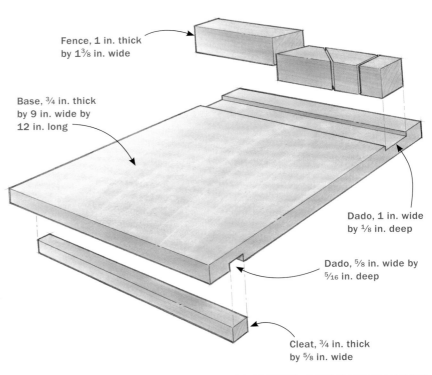

Fence, 1 in. thick by 1⅜ in. wide

Base, ¾ in. thick by 9 in. wide by 12 in. long

Dado, 1 in. wide by ⅛ in. deep

Dado, ⅝ in. wide by ⁵⁄₁₆ in. deep

Cleat, ¾ in. thick by ⅝ in. wide

Saw block for small parts

For small, thin stock, I replace the bigger saw hook with a simple rabbeted block that gets clamped in my vise. I use a Japanese pull saw for trim work, so I orient the block with the fence toward me (reverse that for a Western saw). To make the kerfs, I use the saw itself in combination with a square for alignment.

Extra Help for Holding Work

CHRIS GOCHNOUR

Every piece of furniture I make begins at my workbench and ends there, too. It's where I lay out, cut, and fit joinery, plane surfaces, and glue it all together. At the end of the project, it's where I do things like break edges and look for small defects in the surface. Because the bench is such an important tool, it's critical that it be set up for effective and efficient work. This means it must be able to hold work reliably and securely, while still being flexible enough to get a handle on any part you throw its way.

Front vise. A single-screw vise can rack when you hold a part on one side of the jaw. It also has trouble holding wide or long stock.

Wedge eliminates racking. To prevent racking when clamping a workpiece on one side of the jaw, use an L-shaped wedge. Slide it in from the opposite side so that both sides are clamping something of the same thickness. The vise holds the part securely, and you can work more accurately.

A bench's ability to hold work securely begins with its vises, but it shouldn't be limited by them. When my front and tail vises are unable to get an adequate grip on a workpiece, I turn to other strategies. Most of them involve a holdfast or two. Holdfasts are quick to use, apply plenty of clamping pressure, and can be located just about anywhere on a bench where you can drill a hole. I'll show you how I use them to supplement my vises, as well as a few other techniques that expand my bench's workholding abilities.

Make your vises work better

My bench has a front vise with a wooden jaw, and a traditional tail vise. Both are great, but they have limitations. Luckily, there are simple ways to improve their versatility and effectiveness.

The front vise has a single screw in the center. Almost any time a workpiece is held vertically it is placed to one side of the screw, which causes the jaw to rack and weakens the vise's grip. To prevent racking, make a wedge that slides into the other side of the vise. Once the wedge's thickness matches the workpiece's thickness, you can tighten the vise without racking.

Holdfast extends the grip. Dog holes drilled along the front apron make the front vise more versatile, letting you use it in conjunction with a holdfast to clamp a wide panel for dovetailing. Without the holdfast, the board would chatter so much that sawing would be nearly impossible. A holdfast can also be used to secure the far end of a long board for edge-planing, another task that's far more difficult without the holdfast.

Tail vise. A bit of workholding ingenuity allows you to use your tail vise for more than just face planing.

L-brackets spread the pressure. Benchdogs have trouble clamping wide parts like drawers. Gochnour expands their reach with L-shaped MDF cauls, which stabilize drawers better than straight cauls would. Tighten the drawer between the two cauls and you can plane the drawer's edge without it skittering across the bench or chattering beneath the blade.

Another problem with a single-screw vise is presented by wide boards and panels. A board more than a few inches wider than the side of the jaw can be loose enough that it chatters when you saw dovetails or plane end grain. A holdfast stops the chatter. Knocked into a hole in the front apron, the holdfast locks down the side of the workpiece that's not in the vise. This works great for long boards that need edge-planing, too. Rest the

Plane thin stock without a stop. Planing a thin board against a stop is tricky, because it can bow up under the plane. Gochnour secures the board at the back instead. He clamps a hand screw in the tail vise, then clamps the board in the hand screw. Finally, he planes away from the vise and hand screw.

Holdfasts lock parts down flat. A holdfast excels at securing a part where a vise simply can't reach. When chopping the waste from dovetails, the workpiece must be flat on the benchtop. A holdfast works faster than a bar clamp and can put pressure right where you need it. Whack it on top to lock it down, but on the side to release.

Help with molding an edge. The jaw of a front vise is often in the way of the fence on a combination or molding plane. Clear planing is possible if you pinch the workpiece between dogs and use battens secured by holdfasts to counteract the sideways pressure applied when you plane.

board against the bench's front edge and lock the pad down on the board's face. Now you can plane without the board wobbling.

A tail vise works in tandem with benchdogs for planing parts. But drawers are tough to hold with dogs. I've come up with two solutions. When I need to plane the top or bottom edges of a drawer, I use two simple, L-shaped cauls made from MDF. Used with the tail vise and benchdogs, they spread the clamping pressure over the entire width of the drawer, stabilizing it.

The other solution gets called into action when I need to plane the outside faces of the drawer sides. I made a holding jig with two supports that stretch out in front of the bench and are clamped to the benchtop using holdfasts (see photos, p. 151). A crossbar links the two supports and prevents them from racking. The distance between the supports is adjustable, so the jig can be used for just about any drawer.

Power-tool assist. Gochnour often uses holdfasts to secure a straightedge when routing dadoes. The holdfasts also lock the workpiece to the bench, making the routing operation more stable. And the holdfasts go on and off quickly.

Hand screw adds stability. For best support, chopping a mortise should take place on the benchtop, not in a vise. After clamping the stile on edge in the hand screw, secure the hand screw to the benchtop with a holdfast (above). A holdfast at the stile's other end stabilizes it all the more. This way, the stile won't deflect or fall over under the force of heavy mallet blows.

Let the holdfast take center stage

When you need to clamp something beyond the reach of your vises, the best solution is again the traditional holdfast. For example, the best way to chop out the waste between dovetails is with the workpiece flat on the benchtop. A vise can't help, but a holdfast will.

When a holdfast or two doesn't suffice, turn to a hand screw. You can use one to stabilize a stile on edge to chop mortises on top of the bench. You can also use one with a tail vise to plane thin boards. Clamp the hand screw in the vise, then clamp the board in the hand screw. Plane away from the hand screw and the board won't flex. It's a great fix for an irritating problem.

Lock drawer sides for planing. Holding big boxes is a challenge for any vise. Gochnour's clever jig, with its parallel supports, lets him plane any size drawer.

How it works. Locate the first support so there's just enough room between it and the jaw of the front vise for the drawer front or back to slide in. Add the crossbar and tighten the wedge on the first support. Fit the drawer over the supports, snug up the second support, and tighten the second wedge. The crossbar keeps the supports parallel and prevents them from moving under pressure of planing.

Better than a vise. After the fixture is set up, you can quickly move between sides of the drawer box, and from one drawer to another as long as they are the same size.

Lock down the second support. You should be able to barely slide the drawer onto the supports. Gochnour uses a Veritas Fast-Action Hold-Down to lock the drawer to the support, which prevents the back end from lifting up as you complete a pass with the plane.

Make Short Work of Small Parts

MATT KENNEY

Planing Stop

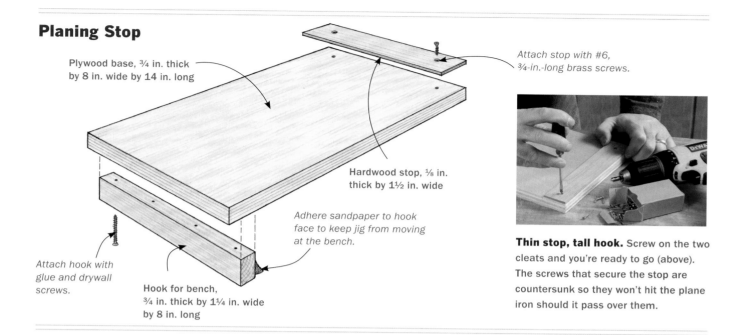

Plywood base, ¾ in. thick by 8 in. wide by 14 in. long

Attach stop with #6, ¾-in.-long brass screws.

Hardwood stop, ⅛ in. thick by 1½ in. wide

Adhere sandpaper to hook face to keep jig from moving at the bench.

Attach hook with glue and drywall screws.

Hook for bench, ¾ in. thick by 1¼ in. wide by 8 in. long

Thin stop, tall hook. Screw on the two cleats and you're ready to go (above). The screws that secure the stop are countersunk so they won't hit the plane iron should it pass over them.

A fter years of making small boxes with delicate trays and cabinets with small drawers, I've found that the safest, fastest, and most precise way to make and fit small parts is with a backsaw, a handplane, and three bench jigs. The jigs—a planing stop, a saw hook, and a shooting board—are easy to make, last a long time, and come in handy for a wide range of jobs.

Each of these jigs is useful by itself, but they really shine when used together. I line them up on my bench and go quickly from one to the next. It makes for a quiet, safe, and efficient workstation. And the fit and finish of my small parts is better than ever.

I'll show you how to make the jigs—and then how to use them—as I make and fit the parts for a jewelry box.

A planing stop for thin stock

This planing jig provides rock-solid support for handplaning small parts, from miter keys to box lids. The base hooks over the edge of the workbench while the ⅛-in.-thick stop prevents the workpiece from sliding. Its low profile won't interfere with thin stock, and

Surface small parts easily. After bandsawing or tablesawing small stock to size, the first step is to remove the saw marks and plane them to thickness. A great job for the planing stop is bringing corner keys to thickness (left). Handplaning is the ideal way to sneak up on a perfect fit (right).

Smooth thin panels and refine joinery. Box lids and other thin panels are easily surfaced at the planing stop (left). With the edge of the panel overhanging the jig, fine-tuning a rabbet is simple and accurate (right).

it's secured with brass screws, which will do less damage if they contact the plane iron. A strip of P220-grit paper on the hardwood hook keeps the jig from sliding sideways. I use high-quality veneer-core plywood for all three jigs, because it stays flat over the long haul.

A versatile saw hook

Like the planing jig, the saw hook is designed to sit on a workbench, providing a stable platform for rough-cutting small parts to length—more quickly and safely than a power tool. Instead of a shallow stop, it has a taller fence that holds the workpiece steady. The fence has 90° and 45° kerfs that guide the sawblade. When making the jig, don't worry

Saw Hook

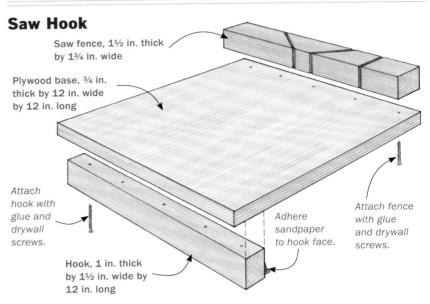

Saw fence, 1½ in. thick by 1¾ in. wide

Plywood base, ¾ in. thick by 12 in. wide by 12 in. long

Attach hook with glue and drywall screws.

Hook, 1 in. thick by 1½ in. wide by 12 in. long

Adhere sandpaper to hook face.

Attach fence with glue and drywall screws.

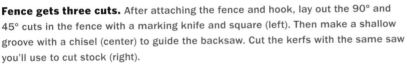

Fence gets three cuts. After attaching the fence and hook, lay out the 90° and 45° cuts in the fence with a marking knife and square (left). Then make a shallow groove with a chisel (center) to guide the backsaw. Cut the kerfs with the same saw you'll use to cut stock (right).

Cut them to length. With the parts smooth and straight, rough them quickly to length on the saw hook. For the sides of this jewelry tray, Kenney measured directly from the workpiece (left), then cut the parts at the saw hook (right). Generally, it's best to leave the pieces a little long and then square the ends and fine-tune the fit at the shooting board (see the facing page).

45° too. The same goes for miters. Here, Kenney trims the waste off the corner keys he planed on the previous page.

Shooting Board

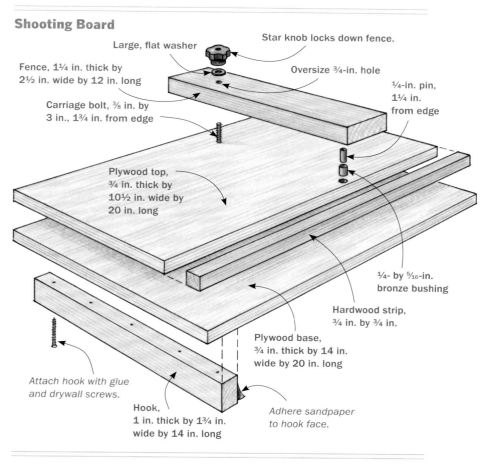

Star knob locks down fence.

Large, flat washer

Fence, 1¼ in. thick by 2½ in. wide by 12 in. long

Carriage bolt, ⅜ in. by 3 in., 1¾ in. from edge

Oversize ¾-in. hole

¼-in. pin, 1¼ in. from edge

Plywood top, ¾ in. thick by 10½ in. wide by 20 in. long

¼- by ⁵⁄₁₆-in. bronze bushing

Hardwood strip, ¾ in. by ¾ in.

Plywood base, ¾ in. thick by 14 in. wide by 20 in. long

Attach hook with glue and drywall screws.

Hook, 1 in. thick by 1¾ in. wide by 14 in. long

Adhere sandpaper to hook face.

Adjustable fence will always be true.
A ¼-in. (I.D.) bronze bushing (top) and a tight-fitting steel pin serve as the pivot point for the fixed end of the fence. The adjustable end has an oversize hole that fits over a carriage bolt (center). Once squared, the fence is locked down with a threaded knob (above).

too much about getting the sawkerfs perfect. This jig is only meant to get parts close to the right length and angle. For a perfect fit, use a low-angle plane and a shooting board.

Shooting board is the most valuable jig

Of all these jigs, the shooting board is the most versatile. You can use it to square up ends, plane miters, and trim parts for a perfect fit. The base is made from a two-piece stack of ¾-in.-thick plywood with the bottom piece about 3 in. wider than the top piece.

With the left sides aligned, the resulting rabbet becomes the runway for the plane. A 3-in. rabbet works for the Veritas low-angle jack plane shown here, but it should be adjusted so it's about 1 in. wider than the height of the plane you'll be using.

A strip of ½-in.-thick hardwood glued to the left side of the rabbet keeps the plane blade from cutting into the plywood (which would dull it). And since the plane blade is not as wide as the plane body, it leaves a narrow ridge of hardwood at the bottom of the runway. The ridge works as a depth stop to keep the blade from reaching and endlessly shaving away the hardwood strip.

Whenever you sharpen your jack plane, you'll need to trim away the ridge with a shoulder plane and then re-establish a new ridge with the newly sharpened jack plane.

Now fine-tune the fit. After you've planed your pieces smooth and sawn them to rough length, the shooting board does the really important work, such as planing ends and edges square. After aligning the opposite ends, squaring pairs of parts at the same time ensures they're exactly the same length.

The perfect fit. With the workpiece slightly oversize, plane one end square and then take a pass or two on the opposite end. Continue planing and test-fitting until you get a snug fit.

Joint edges safely. You can joint the long sides of small parts at the shooting board, too. And it's safer than a jointer.

Make Perfect miters

By adding a 45° auxiliary fence to the shooting board, you can make tight miters with minimal fuss.

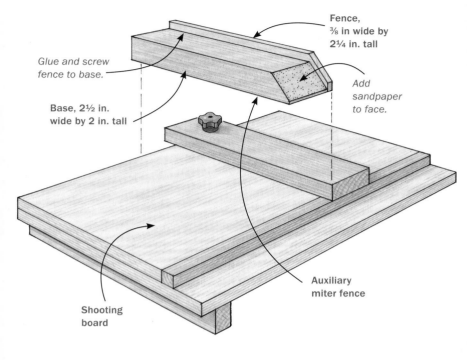

Fence, ⅜ in wide by 2¼ in. tall

Glue and screw fence to base.

Add sandpaper to face.

Base, 2½ in. wide by 2 in. tall

Auxiliary miter fence

Shooting board

Simple jig makes miters too. Clamp the miter jig to the shooting board's fence, so it doesn't shift sideways.

Plane the miter. A firm grip and P220-grit sandpaper glued to the jig prevent the stock from moving as the miter is planed perfectly true.

Get a Grip on Your Work

JOHN PARKINSON

Nothing more than a steel rod with a bend in it and a flattened pad at one end, the holdfast has been treasured in the woodshop for more than 300 years as a simple, quick, and effective method for holding work on the bench. All you need is a perfectly located hole in your benchtop. Drop the holdfast into the hole with the workpiece under its arm. Whack the holdfast from above to lock it in place and secure the work. Time to remove it? Knock it on the stem and it comes loose. It's that easy. I'll show you some ins and outs, along with a few examples of the holdfast's versatile workholding abilities.

Easy on, easy off. A sharp hit just in front of the bend wedges the holdfast securely in the hole. Another pop with the mallet, this time on the back of the stem, releases the pressure.

The ideal clamp for benchwork. The holdfast's offset stem and low-profile pad allow you to get pressure close to where the work is happening without getting in the way. The key is finding the right spots to drill holes for it (see p. 162). Whether you're paring dovetails (facing page) or chopping mortises (above), a single holdfast is often enough to prevent the workpiece from moving under the force of the chisel.

An extra hand for jigs. It takes more than a cleat on the underside of a sawhook or shooting board to keep it steady during use. A holdfast on top of the fence eliminates all movement.

Never in the way. Unlike clamps, holdfasts don't hang off the front of the bench, which means you can position them so that they don't interfere with the work at hand.

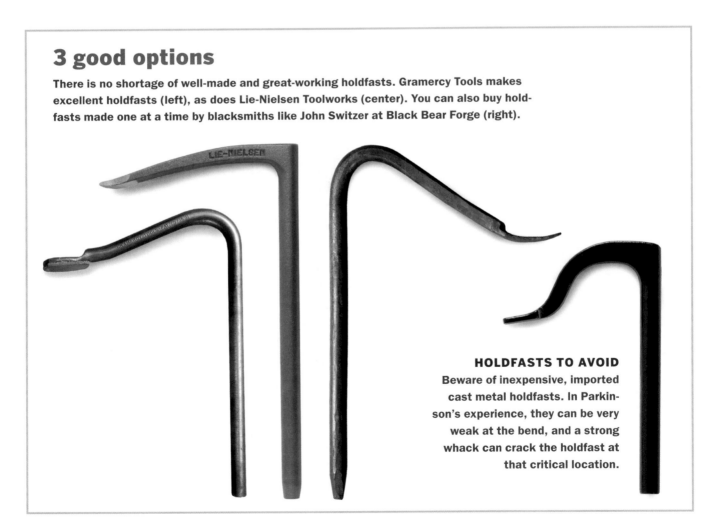

3 good options

There is no shortage of well-made and great-working holdfasts. Gramercy Tools makes excellent holdfasts (left), as does Lie-Nielsen Toolworks (center). You can also buy holdfasts made one at a time by blacksmiths like John Switzer at Black Bear Forge (right).

HOLDFASTS TO AVOID
Beware of inexpensive, imported cast metal holdfasts. In Parkinson's experience, they can be very weak at the bend, and a strong whack can crack the holdfast at that critical location.

A strong arm for handwork

Simplicity is part of what makes the holdfast so great. Inserted into a hole slightly bigger than the diameter of its shaft, the holdfast wedges into the hole when struck from above. Smack it on the back and it's no longer wedged. The speed and simplicity of the process encourages you to adjust the holdfast repeatedly as you're working so that you can orient the workpiece for more efficient chopping, planing, paring, or sawing.

Because the holdfast's stem is offset from the workpiece, it's rarely in the way of your tool. The clamping pad is low profile as well. You can place it close to the action and not worry about hitting it with a chisel or plane. Try that with an F-clamp.

For such a simple tool, the holdfast applies a tremendous amount of clamping pressure. Under its grip, a workpiece or jig simply won't move, and this makes working with hand tools easier and safer.

Now you need some holes

To use a holdfast, you need a hole through your benchtop. The key is making sure the holes are drilled square to the surface.

I've found that the easiest and safest way to drill holes for a holdfast is with another

Protect your work. One downside to holdfasts is that their steel pads can dent the workpiece. To prevent this type of damage, put a more forgiving material, between the pad and workpiece. Soft enough to prevent damage but dense enough to transfer the holdfast's pressure, leather is the perfect material to cover a pad. Glue it on, and you'll never need to go looking for it.

centuries-old tool, a brace equipped with an auger bit. Used in conjunction with a guide block, it drills a hole 90° to the surface of the benchtop with no trouble.

To make the guide, mill up a piece of stock at least 2 in. thick and long enough to reach

Wood makes a good pad, too. A piece of scrap would work, but a dedicated pad stays with the holdfast and spreads out the pressure a bit.

Holes only where you need them

It's not a good idea to create holes willy-nilly in the benchtop. First identify the area on the bench where you perform a task, such as chopping mortises or shooting end grain, and drill a hole that will locate the holdfast in the best place to assist in the job.

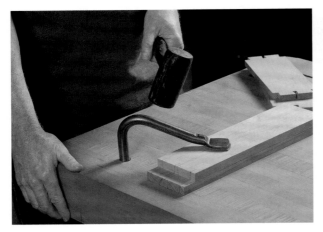

Near a leg for mortises and dovetails

In the center for shooting boards, sawhooks, and other jigs.

Along the front edge for long, narrow work, or tough-to-clamp jigs like a benchtop vise.

TIP Don't forget the front. Holes in the leg opposite the front vise allow you to stabilize workpieces that are too long for the vise alone.

How and where to drill. Be thoughtful when drilling holes in your bench for the stem. Locate them where you do most of your handwork. A brace and bit work best for drilling. An auger bit moves quickly but leaves a nice hole. A drilling guide, made at a drill press and clamped to the bench, ensures that the holes are square to the surface.

more than halfway across the top's width. At the drill press, drill a hole through the guide. As I mentioned, for the holdfast to work properly, the diameter of the hole should be slighter larger than the diameter of the holdfast's stem— ¾ in. dia. in most cases.

Before you drill the holes, plan out where to put them. To do this, think of how you work. When you pound on a mortise chisel to clear waste from a mortise, you're working over a leg. So, you need a hole offset from the leg that allows the holdfast's pad to land on the workpiece. Put any jigs you use (shooting board, saw hook) on the bench where you use them. Locate the hole so that the holdfast can lock down the jig without being in the way. Work

through all the other tasks that need a holdfast and you'll identify where to put the holes.

To drill the holes, clamp the guide to your bench, put an auger bit in your brace, and drop the bit into the guide's hole. Depending on the thickness of the top and the length of the bit, you might need to stop partway through and remove the guide to drill all the way through the top. The hole in the top serves as a guide for the remainder of the cut.

Clever Clamping Tricks

TIMOTHY COLEMAN

Ifind myself continually reaching for a couple of ordinary clamps to address many unusual holding needs. Whenever I need to hold an odd-shaped part and can't justify the time to make a dedicated jig, these two simple, versatile tools, the

wooden hand-screw clamp and the wooden cam clamp, are invaluable.

My favorite hand-screw clamp has jaws 12 in. long that open almost 9 in. I often use it on my workbench, clamped between the benchdogs or in the tail vise or shoulder

Versatility at hand. Wooden hand screws and cam clamps, available from many sources, provide inventive options for holding unusual workpieces. Hand screws, with hefty jaws that can be angled, will grip tapered parts. Cam clamps deliver moderate pressure with lightness and speed.

vise. It's especially helpful for holding a part above the bench surface to give more hand clearance when I'm carving or using a spokeshave. The hand screw's jaws can be angled to each other, so it can easily grip many tapered objects that benchdogs couldn't handle. Because the jaws are wood, they're more friendly to an errant carving tool or router bit. The heft of the hand screw and the flat faces of its jaws provide stability on the bench.

Cam clamps don't have huge holding power, but they are light, slender, and very easy and quick to use. Like hand screws, they have flat-sided jaws that make it easy to clamp them to other surfaces; because the cam clamp's jaws are thinner, they can be useful in situations where hand screws are too big. And because the cam clamp's jaws are made of wood, it's possible to modify them or tack other parts onto them for some operations.

Both hand screws and cam clamps are great at the workbench, but they are just as useful and versatile for machine work. I'll use them to hold a part still for joinery or shaping, or as a kind of carriage to hold a part while I slide the clamp along the machine table to make a cut. Finding elegant solutions to tricky problems is the part of furniture making that makes me most satisfied.

Get a handle on traditional clamps

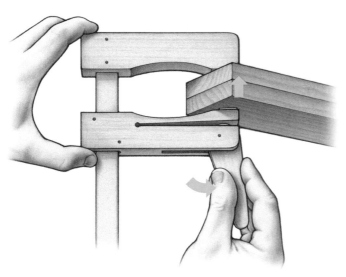

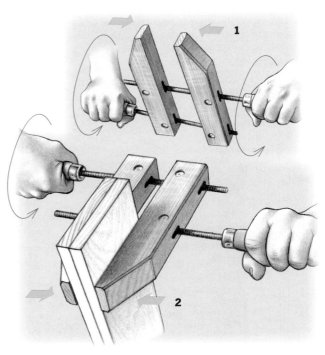

CAM CLAMPS

The cam clamp is activated by flipping forward a cam on the movable jaw. Most cam clamps have cork pads on their jaws to avoid marring the workpiece.

HAND-SCREW CLAMPS

Opening or closing a hand-screw clamp is like riding a bicycle: Once you know how to do it, you're off to the races. Hold the handles and crank them as though you are hand-cranking the pedals of an inverted bicycle. The clamp will open or close in a blur (1). To exert pressure with the tips of a hand screw, always open the back screw rather than tightening the front screw (2).

Clamp odd shapes for handwork

Hand-screw clamps are an irreplaceable supplement to the vises on a workbench. Whether gripped between benchdogs, held in one of the vises, or fixed in place with a quick-release clamp, a hand screw offers a means to grip all sorts of curved, tapered, and irregular parts for hand shaping.

The right grip for curved parts. A hand-screw clamp pinched in the tail vise provides a versatile means of holding a curved workpiece for shaping. By elevating one end of the part, the clamp provides hand clearance and access to the sides.

Stabilize a plank. You can use a hand screw to hold tall boards tight for planing or shaping the top edge. A clamp holds the hand screw firmly flat to the bench.

Hold tapers tight. The hand screw's jaws can be quickly adjusted to grip a wedge-shaped workpiece. Here Coleman uses benchdogs to clamp the hand screw in place.

Any table becomes a bench. Hand screws and cam clamps make a quick improvised vise on most any surface in the shop.

Odd shapes, exposed ends. The hand screw's jaws can grip all sorts of unusual shapes, and it also lifts the workpiece, exposing its ends for shaping.

Wooden clamps amp up the router

The hand screw's versatility is especially evident when it's paired with a router. It can hold an unusual workpiece still, it can hold the router itself, or it can be used as a carriage, moving the workpiece across a router table while holding an odd-shaped piece at an angle. Cam clamps, too, pair well with routers.

Stable but slender. Like hand screws, cam clamps have flat-sided jaws that lie nicely on the bench. Their jaws are narrow, making them the right choice here, as they pinch a workpiece by its tenons without getting in the way of the router.

Routing a wedge-shaped workpiece. While template routing, Coleman uses a hand-screw clamp to hold a small, tapered workpiece that affords no extra space for hold-downs.

Instant router table. For routing small parts, Coleman uses an inverted trim router. He locks the router in place with a hand screw, and fixes the hand screw to the bench with a clamp.

Carriage for a curved part. To rout a slot in the end of a curved part, Coleman grips it with a hand screw and moves the clamp across the table to make the cut.

Of clamps and machines

Hand screws and cam clamps are very useful for machine work. Although it's best to cut the joinery on shaped parts while they are still rectilinear blanks, sometimes that's not practical. In those cases, wooden clamps can provide an alternative to building a complicated fixture for cutting joinery on an oddly shaped part.

Holding tight to a sinuous workpiece. To mortise the end of an S-shaped chair arm, Coleman uses a cam clamp in conjunction with his slot mortiser's hold-down. To provide a support for the part at the proper angle, he tacked a scrap across the jaws of the clamp.

Bandsaw work at a challenging angle. Using the hand screw as a carriage enables Coleman to accurately and safely make a curved end cut on a curved workpiece.

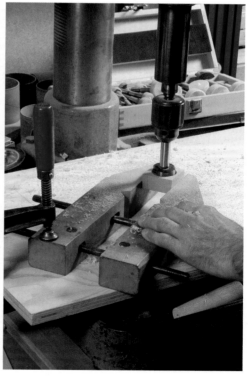

Pinching a tiny part. Drilling into a small part with a high-torque bit can be dangerous. Here, Coleman uses a hand screw clamped to the drill-press table to hold a small workpiece safely for drilling with a Forstner bit.

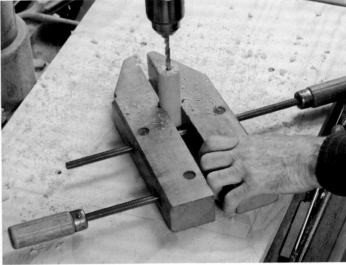

A tricky bit of drilling. The mating pair of notches Coleman cut into the jaws of his hand-screw clamp hold a dowel tight and upright for end-grain drilling.

Suction where you want it. Coleman uses a hand screw and some cam clamps to hold the dust-collection hose just where he needs it.

Shopmade "Bench Puppies"

TIMOTHY COLEMAN

My workbench is one of the most valuable tools in my shop. It is a traditional European design and, with a few accessories, it has served me well for nearly 30 years. One accessory that I reach for often is a pair of shopmade jaws that slip into the dog holes in the benchtop and tail vise to clamp a workpiece on edge. I was introduced to these devices as a student at the College of the Redwoods, where they were affectionately known as "bench puppies."

These helpers are about as simple as it gets when it comes to bench jigs. They're made from scrap hardwood and a dowel, with a cork cushion glued to the clamping faces to protect the workpiece as the puppies bite down.

The problem with a tail vise is that its grip is limited. It often leaves one end of a workpiece unsupported, and it doesn't easily hold odd-shaped pieces or drawers for planing. Bench puppies step in to stretch the clamping limits of the tail vise. They grab both ends of the workpiece and hold it against the front of the bench. They'll hold any shape workpiece, whether it's a long board that needs edge-planing, a door that needs fitting, or an odd-shaped piece that needs fine-tuning with hand tools. They even grip drawers securely.

The hardest part about making them is putting the dowel in the right spot. The location will vary based on the distance between the dog holes and the front edge of your bench. You'll also need to make two of them,

The gift of grab

Used in conjunction with a tail vise, bench puppies can hold any size or shape workpiece against the front of the bench. Insert one puppy in a benchtop dog hole, hold the work against it, then insert the opposite puppy in a tail vise dog hole and tighten.

Edge-planing

Drawers

Odd shapes

Bench puppy

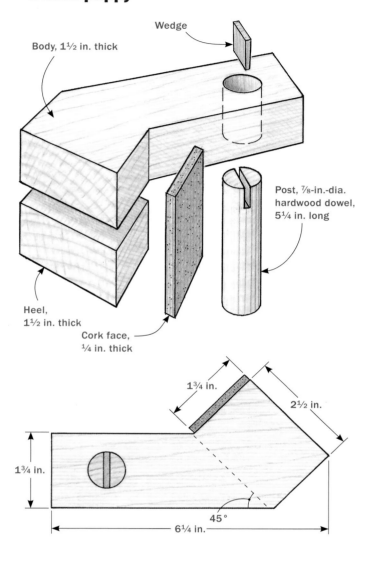

Wedge

Body, 1½ in. thick

Heel,
1½ in. thick

Cork face,
¼ in. thick

Post, ⅞-in.-dia.
hardwood dowel,
5¼ in. long

1¾ in.

2½ in.

1¾ in.

6¼ in.

45°

Locate the post hole

The post anchors the puppy in the workbench's dog hole. Because the dog-hole placement varies from bench to bench, you'll have to figure out the dowel location yourself. Fortunately, it's not difficult. Start with a full-size plan view of the puppy, then follow the steps below.

STEP 1
Mark centerline.

STEP 2
Extend a 45° line
from inside corner.

STEP 4
Mark dowel location
at intersection.

STEP 3
Measure from edge of bench to center
of benchdog hole (photo above) and
plot a line parallel to the 45° line.

a right- and left-hand puppy. Make sure you label each one, so you don't end up with two righties or two lefties.

Start with two hardwood blocks for each puppy, one for the body and one for the heel. Use a full-size drawing to lay out the shape on the body, and to mark for the dowel location. Cut out the shape on the bandsaw and drill the hole using a Forstner bit. Glue the heel to the body, and then add the dowel

and wedge. You don't have to spend a lot of time sanding the body. I simply break the hard corners with a sanding block. Finally, glue the cork pad to the jaw. You can get cork from almost any office-supply store. That's it. The puppies are ready for business.

Once you've made and used these, you will have reached clamping nirvana.

Assemble the body. The process begins with two hardwood blanks for each puppy—one for the body and one for the heel.

Cut the body to shape. All the cuts are easily made on the bandsaw. Make the angled cuts first (left), then use a fence to finish the straight inside cut (above).

Drill for the post. The post anchors the puppy in the benchdog hole. Transfer its location from the plan and then drill the hole for it using a Forstner bit.

Glue the heel to the body. Be careful at this stage. Make sure you don't make two righties or two lefties. You want one of each.

Add the post. The post is a store-bought hardwood dowel that gets glued and wedged into the body of the puppy. The post is slotted on one end for the wedge that anchors it to the body. To support the post for the slotting cut, Coleman uses a cradle made from a scrap block (top). After marking the stopping point of the cut on the top face of the cradle, he inserts the post and uses the bandsaw fence to ensure a straight cut (above).

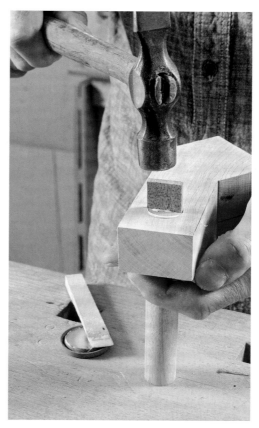

Glue it in. Be sure to orient the slot perpendicular to the grain of the body so that you don't split it when you drive in the wedge.

Add the jaw pad. Glue and clamp the cork face to the jaw of the puppy. A light sanding to break the hard corners is all that's left before you can put the jigs to work.

The Versatile Wedge

BOB VAN DYKE

The wedge: I'm continually amazed at how something so simple can be so incredibly useful. It's common to see wedges used in joinery, and they are the traditional way that a cutter is held in a hand tool like a handplane or cutting gauge. But I also find them really handy in certain clamping situations where traditional clamps are cumbersome or completely ineffective.

Not only is the force created by wedging action great when used to hold parts together, but that same force can also be used to safely separate parts with no damage.

How to make them

Need just a couple? Go freehand

Lay out the wedges on a board and bandsaw to your pencil lines. These freehand wedges typically need smoothing with a handplane. Clamping them together in the vise for planing keeps the angles identical.

Need a bunch? Make a jig

Cut a notch the size and shape of the wedge you need in a piece of ¾-in.-thick MDF or plywood. Place the wedge stock in the notch and run the jig along the bandsaw's fence. Flip the workpiece end over end after each cut.

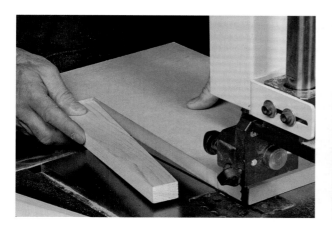

How to clamp thin panels with wedges. This jig clamps thin stock together by squeezing it between two fences with a wedge. It can be scaled up or down to match the size of any project.

Build the jig. Screw one fence to a piece of ¾-in.-thick plywood (top). To keep from gluing your workpieces to the jig, add packing tape to the top of the base. Then set the workpiece and wedge in place, and screw on the other fence (above).

I constantly find new purposes for wedges in the shop, even though they've been around as long as recorded history. Here I'll show a few ways to clamp with wedges, a few ways to take things apart, and a few ways to hold work at the bench. Once you've explored all the ways wedges can help you in the shop, you may think twice about buying another expensive specialty clamp.

They are easy to make

If you save offcuts from angled furniture parts like tapered legs, you might already have ready-made wedges stashed around your shop. When I need a wedge that's a certain size or with a specific slope, it's easy to cut one or two wedges from the edge of a board on the bandsaw.

When I need multiple wedges of the same size and shape, I cut them on the bandsaw

Ready to work. With the two fences in place, glue the edges of the workpieces and get them into position (left). A few light taps on the end of the wedge clamps this panel together (below). You can keep the pieces from springing up under the pressure by resting something heavy on top, like a handplane.

with a simple jig (see photos, p 177). Plane the stock to thickness and cut it to length, then place it in the jig's notch and push it through the blade. Flip the stock end over end to cut the next wedge. For most clamping applications these bandsawn wedges will be ready to use right off the saw.

But if the bandsaw leaves too rough a surface, clamp the wedges together in a vise and smooth them with a handplane.

To make wedges on a tablesaw, use a taper jig. Select a wide rectangular workpiece and set the fence to produce a tapered offcut just the size you want for your wedge. The type

Edging. With some help from a clamp across the end, you can use long, thin wedges to clamp edging onto the end of a countertop that's too long for your clamps to span.

of wood used does not usually matter, but if there is a chance that the wedge could damage my work, I make it from a softwood like pine. Wedges are usually cut with the grain running down the length—wedges cut across the grain are likely to break when driven in.

Handle unique glue-ups

Wedges are perfect for joining small pieces and for other glue-ups that can be frustrating with conventional clamps. For instance, when edge-gluing wood to make thin door panels and small box tops, the pieces are difficult to keep flat in bar clamps, and sometimes the clamps just won't stay on.

To get around the problem, I use wedges and a simple fixture that's quick to make from scraps, screws, and packing tape. Cut

Even pressure on edging. A pine caul on each side helps line up the trim flush with the edges (top left). Add a clamp across the end of the counter (left), spacing the bar about ¼ in. from the wood edging. Tap in wedges (above) to apply pressure evenly along the glue joint.

two fences at least as thick and a little longer than the pieces to be glued, and wide enough that they won't flex under pressure—2 in. wide usually works. Make the base from a scrap of ¾-in.-thick plywood wide enough to hold the two fences, a wedge, and the parts to be glued. To keep glue from sticking to the base, I put packing tape on the top surface of the plywood.

Screw one of the fences to the base and place the panels to be glued up side by side against it. Place a wedge longer than the workpiece next to it. Slide the opposing fence against the wedge and screw it in place. Remove the workpieces, glue the edges, put them back between the fences, and then tap in the wedge. The wedge will lock them in place and apply even pressure across the entire joint. To keep the pieces of the panel from springing up under pressure, stack a caul and a heavy object like a handplane on top.

Gluing edging to the end of a long counter-top is another task made simple by wedges. I don't often have clamps long enough to reach the length of a countertop, so I place a bar clamp across the end and leave a small gap between the bar and the workpiece. Then I insert wedges between the clamp and the edging. Put glue on the edging and slip it in place, then add the clamp and tap in enough wedges from top and bottom to exert even pressure.

Hold work at the bench

I use an assortment of wedges at my bench to support or hold furniture parts. The wedges work great and don't get in the way like a clamp might. One way I use them is to stabilize parts that aren't flat, like a cupped board. I also place a wedge under a shaped part, like a tapered leg, so it won't rock as I plane it. For routing, I use a simple jig, clamping the work with opposing wedges.

Clamping stock in a bench vise for edge-planing is another task that can be awkward,

Hold work. Wedges are great at helping secure stock at the bench. Save offcuts to use as benchtop shims and build a simple jig to make edge-planing and routing easy. Use wedges to stabilize a cupped board or an oddly shaped workpiece on the workbench.

For edge-planing a wedged bird's mouth holds tight. Slide the workpiece into the bird's mouth along with the hooked wedge. The force of planing will tighten the wedge's grip. Release the board by tapping on its end (right).

For routing wedges won't get in the way. Opposing wedges can clamp work for routing. Van Dyke uses a U-shaped jig to hold the workpiece for mortising and to support the router. A pair of wedges anchors the work solidly in the jig.

especially with long boards in situations where the ends are unsupported. A bird's-mouth jig with a wedge makes this job easy because the entire length of the board is supported on the benchtop. To use it just push the end of the board into the bird's mouth with the hooked wedge, and the piece will be held tight. To release it, just give it a tap on the end.

Disassemble without damaging

Long, low-angle wedges are perfect for separating parts that have been temporarily joined with double-sided tape, like a flush-cutting router template. To separate tight dovetails in a dry-assembled box while keeping the two sides parallel, you can drive wide opposing wedges between the two sides. You can use thin, low-angle wedges

to disassemble furniture for repairs, too. Carefully drive them in to separate stubborn old glued-up parts for repair without further damaging the piece.

Try a few of these techniques, and it might just spark your imagination to come up with other ways to put wedges to work.

Take it apart. How many times have you been frustrated when trying to get templates off workpieces or disassembling a dry-fitted drawer? Wedges are the solution. Use them to take off a stuck-on template. A router template attached with double-sided tape isn't always easy to get apart. Drive in wedges to separate the pieces.

Safely separate stubborn dovetails. Two large opposing wedges force the sides apart while keeping them parallel, so there's no chance of cracking a pin.

Put down the pry bar. When the glue in those tired old furniture joints gives out, wedges do a great job getting them apart for repair without marring the wood.

All-in-One Workstation for Dovetails

MICHAEL PEKOVICH

My work tends to require a lot of dovetailing, in white oak no less, which can be a chore. Because of that, one technique I've adopted to speed the process and save some wear on my chisels is to rout out the waste between the pins. To help with that, I made a simple stand to support the work vertically and provide a flat horizontal surface for the router to rest on. While this use alone makes it worth building, the stand can handle a number of other dovetailing jobs as well. In fact, if you don't own a bench with a vise, this stand can assist you through the entire process. If you have a sturdy work table and a couple of clamps, you can be cutting dovetails.

CHOPPING

ROUTING

No workbench? No problem. Although originally intended for routing the waste between dovetail pins, this stand provides a stable platform and secure clamping for tackling a variety of dovetail tasks without the need for a vise.

Work stand for dovetails

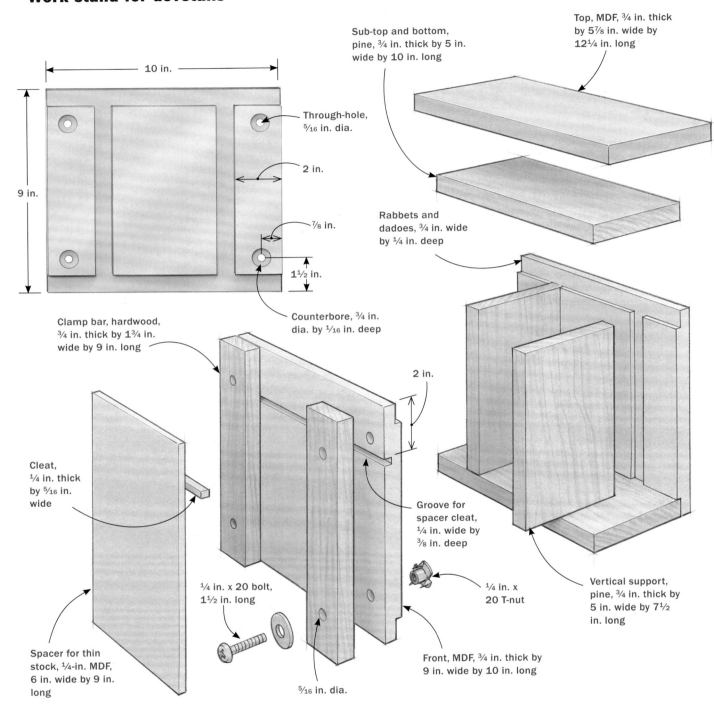

10 in.

9 in.

Sub-top and bottom, pine, ¾ in. thick by 5 in. wide by 10 in. long

Top, MDF, ¾ in. thick by 5⅞ in. wide by 12¼ in. long

Through-hole, 5/16 in. dia.

2 in.

⅞ in.

1½ in.

Rabbets and dadoes, ¾ in. wide by ¼ in. deep

Counterbore, ¾ in. dia. by 1/16 in. deep

Clamp bar, hardwood, ¾ in. thick by 1¾ in. wide by 9 in. long

2 in.

Cleat, ¼ in. thick by 5/16 in. wide

Groove for spacer cleat, ¼ in. wide by ⅜ in. deep

¼ in. x 20 bolt, 1½ in. long

¼ in. x 20 T-nut

Vertical support, pine, ¾ in. thick by 5 in. wide by 7½ in. long

Spacer for thin stock, ¼-in. MDF, 6 in. wide by 9 in. long

5/16 in. dia.

Front, MDF, ¾ in. thick by 9 in. wide by 10 in. long

Unexpected benefits of a smaller stand

The router stand in this article is a smaller version of a design I've been using for years. When I began traveling frequently to teach, the original stand proved too heavy and bulky to bring along. So I set about making a smaller, lighter version inspired in part by a travel stand of Bob Van Dyke's, so credit goes to Bob as well. It performs the basic routing tasks just as well as the larger version, but its small size and lighter weight make it easy to reposition on the bench, and that in turn makes it easy to perform a number of additional tasks. If you flip the stand on its back, the stock can be secured parallel to the benchtop. That allows it to serve as a workstation not just for routing, but also for scribing, sawing, and chopping.

The structure is simple

Made from home center materials, and requiring only a couple of rabbets and dadoes, the stand goes together quickly.

The joinery is there to help keep the parts aligned during assembly and you can skip it altogether if you wish. I used MDF for most of the stand because of its flatness and stability, but I went with pine for some parts because of its nail- and screw-holding ability. You'll also need some toggle clamps and T-nuts, which secure the bars the clamps are attached to.

This stand can handle parts up to 6 in. wide between the clamp bars, and you can accommodate up to 10-in.-wide boards by removing one or both bars and using regular clamps to secure the work instead. If you regularly work with wider stock, you may want to make a wider stand. If you do make a wider stand, I would recommend additional rows of T-nuts on the face to allow repositioning of the clamp bars to handle narrow stock as well.

Building a basic box

All of the joinery is cut into the inside faces of the front and rear panels. I use a dado

Rabbets and dadoes keep parts aligned. Use a dado blade to cut the dadoes and rabbets, adding a sacrificial fence for the rabbets. Before assembly, drill the inside face for the T-nuts and tap them in place.

blade to cut the dadoes for the vertical supports as well as the rabbets along the top and bottom edges for the sub-top and bottom. To cut the rabbets, attach a sacrificial fence to the rip fence and set it so the blade just skims it. The front panel is drilled and counterbored for T-nuts to attach the clamp bars.

Glue and nail or screw the base together. I use an 18-gauge brad nailer for the job. After the glue is dry, screw the top in place. Skip glue here in case you need to replace it at some point. Also make sure to drive the screws into the sub-top at the vertical support locations. The top is wider than the base to offer more support for the router when

Assembly is quick. Glue and nail the stand together, then screw on the top without glue. Inset the top from the front face to provide clearance when routing and drive the screws at the vertical support locations.

Add the clamp bars and toggle clamps. The clamp bars are attached with bolts through the T-nuts, so they can be removed easily when working with wider stock. Then the toggle clamps are screwed to the bars.

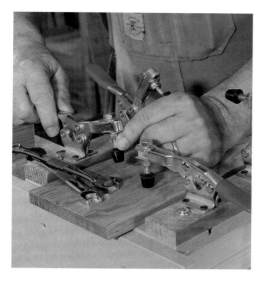

Cutting dovetails. Adjust the clamps to the stock. Loosen the bolts that secure the pads and adjust for a snug fit. Don't over-tighten the clamps; the pressure should be just enough to keep the part from shifting.

you are dovetailing wide pieces. The extra length also makes it easy to clamp the alignment plate in place when positioning the pin stock for routing. The alignment plate is a piece of MDF the same size as the top. I glue a 1/16-in.-thick strip of wood to the underside at the front edge, and that allows me to offset the workpiece 1/16 in. lower than the top when I need to.

The toggle clamps are screwed to clamp bars that bolt to the case. The bars are 3/4 in. thick, which is roughly the same thickness as the case parts and drawer fronts that I tend to dovetail. This ensures that the clamps can be adjusted to secure the workpiece. I add a spacer for thinner stock. Make them out of a hardwood to ensure that the screws won't pull out under clamping pressure.

Clamp the stand vertically for sawing. The stand supports the stock at a comfortable height for sawing the tails and coping the waste in between. Position it proud of the tabletop edge to allow clearance for working with longer parts. Use heavy clamps to keep the stand steady when sawing.

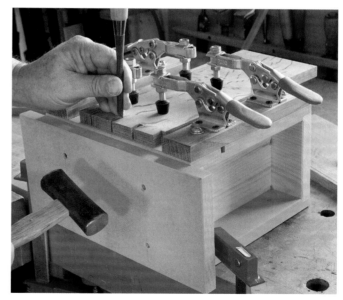

Clamp the stand on its back for chopping. Adjust the stock so that it's supported by the subtop when chopping. This transfers the chopping force directly to the tabletop and provides solid support.

TIP Add a shim for thin stock. When working with stock thinner than the clamp bars, add a shim between the stand and the stock. Glue a cleat to the back of the shim that fits into the groove in the face to secure it when the stand is in the vertical position.

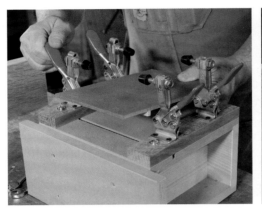 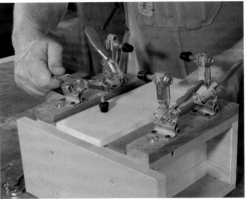

Sawing pins. The stand makes scribing easy. To position the pin board while clamping it, use a flip block. This square block has a strip of wood glued to one face to create a lip to register the work. After clamping the stock (left), place the flip block at the back of the top to support the rear end for scribing (above).

Using the stand

Start by adjusting the toggle clamps to the thickness of the stock. Laying the stand flat on the table makes the process easier. To cut the tails, turn the stand upright and clamp it to a sturdy work surface with its face slightly overhanging the edge of the tabletop.

This will allow you to clamp longer boards in place.

Clamp the stock so it extends above the top and is parallel to it. The stand does a good job of holding the work securely while raising it up to a more comfortable height for sawing. Once the angled cuts are made, I

Saw the pins. Once again, the stand elevates the stock at a good height for sawing and gets the work closer to eye level.

remove most of the waste between the tails with a fretsaw to make chopping easier.

With the waste removed, reposition the stand so its front is facing up and the stock is horizontal. Slide the stock back so that the tails are supported by the stand and chop to the baseline with a chisel. The elevated surface helps while chopping.

Cope out the waste before routing. There's no need to get too close to the scribe line. The router will take care of anything within ¼ in. of the baseline.

TIP Remove the clamp bars for wide stock. By swapping out the toggle clamps for hand clamps, the stand can handle work up to 10 in. wide, which should cover most drawer dovetailing tasks.

Transfer the pin locations

Clamp the stand back in the vertical position to scribe the pins from the tails. For this step I use a flip block, a square length of stock with a strip of wood glued to one face that creates a lip. Pinch the block to the stock with the lip tight to the top edge and lower the stock until the block is resting on the stand top. Now lock down the clamps. Then, to support the rear end of the tail board for scribing, move the block to the rear of the top with the lip overhanging the back edge. Leave the stock in the stand to saw the pins and cope out most of the waste. There's no need to saw too close to the baseline. The router bit will handle any waste under ¼ in. high. I aim for around ⅛ in.,

Rout the waste

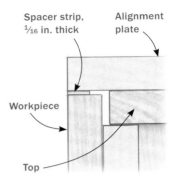

Spacer strip, 1/16 in. thick

Alignment plate

Workpiece

Top

Spacer strip creates gap between the workpiece and router base.

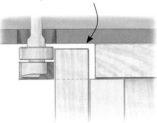

Stock height is critical to an even baseline. Clamp an alignment plate to the stand and snug the workpiece against it while tightening the toggles. Pekovich uses tape on the end grain when dovetailing, so he added a strip to his plate to recess the stock below the surface. This prevents the tape from contacting the router base when routing.

Extralong base keeps the router level. Pekovich replaced the stock router base with a longer base, making it easier to keep the router flat and prevent it from dipping into the cut.

Bearing-guided bit takes the stress out of the process. A short straight bit with a bearing on the shank makes quick work of the waste. The bearing rides against the pin walls and prevents the cutter from cutting into the pins. Adjust the bit depth right to the scribe line and there's no waste left to clean up.

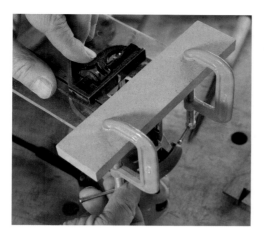

Add a fence to limit the depth of cut.
For half-blind dovetails, clamp a fence to the router base to create the inset for the dovetail socket lap.

Half-blind dovetails

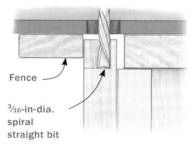

Fence

³⁄₁₆-in-dia. spiral straight bit

which leaves me a little cushion should I stray while sawing.

Routing waste is where the stand shines

Even if you handle every task up to this point at the workbench, this task alone makes the stand worth having. Start by clamping the alignment plate to the stand's top with a spring clamp on each side. The plate should extend ½ in. or so past the front edge of the top. With the flat side of the plate facing down, you can set the stock flush with the top. Or, with the spacer strip side down, you can recess the stock slightly below the top. This is a handy option, because I add tape to

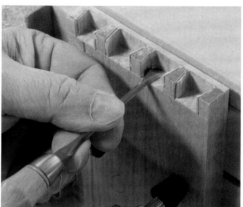

Stay clear of the pins and clean up by hand.
With no bearing to guide the way, you'll have to be careful not to rout into the pins. To clean out the waste after routing, start with a fishtail chisel or a pair of skew chisels and sever the end grain into the corners of the sockets where the router bit can't reach. Then pare the walls with a bench chisel. Leaving the tape in place during this process makes it easier to check your progress.

the ends of the workpiece when scribing and I like to leave it in place while routing so I'll have a good guide for paring where the joint is a little too snug. However, the tape on the end grain can peel up when routing and gum up the bottom of the router base. I avoid this by recessing the stock so that the router base doesn't contact the end of the board.

Use a short bearing-guided bit to rout to the baseline. The bearing on the shank of the bit rides along the sawn walls of the pins and prevents the bit from cutting into them. Set the router bit to the baseline and work your way across the board. After you're finished routing, keep the stock in the stand, raising it up a bit, and pare to fit as needed.

Half-blind dovetails are a little more work

The process is similar to routing regular dovetails, but unfortunately a straight bit is the only option for half-blind dovetails. Again, set the bit depth to hit the baseline. But this time, add a fence to the base to prevent routing past the lap line. Get as close to the sidewalls as you dare, but be prepared to do some chisel work to finish up the corners. Use a pair of skew chisels or a fishtail chisel to sever the end grain in the corners where the router bit couldn't reach, then pare the waste with a bench chisel.

A Shooting Board That Handles 5 Jobs

TIMOTHY ROUSSEAU

As an instructor at the Center for Furniture Craftsmanship, I have seen many different shooting boards through the years. After using them at the school, I often made versions of the best ones for my own shop. They really started to pile up, which bugged me, because I am by nature a distiller, constantly evaluating my tools, machines, jigs, and techniques to find the cleanest and simplest solutions.

The shooting board shown here retired most of the others. Made from one piece of plywood and three pieces of solid wood, it is simple but amazingly versatile, as it can be used for five different planing jobs.

Like most shooting boards, it's good for trimming end grain and miters. But it also works great for shooting the edge of a board and serves as a planing stop, too, handling both thin and thick parts. I'll show you how

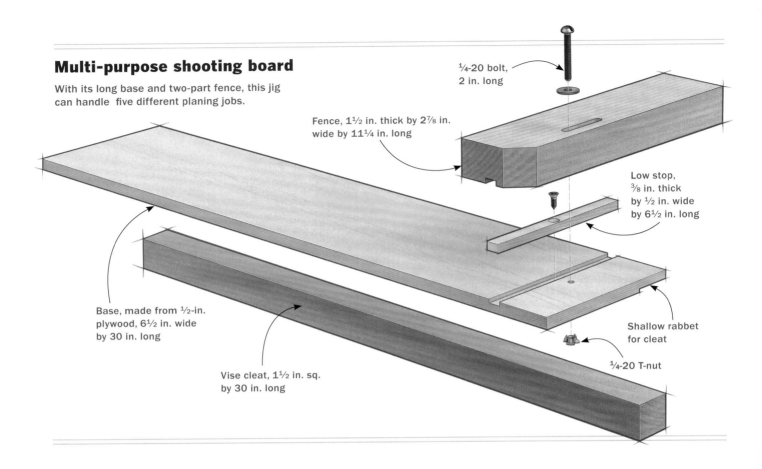

Multi-purpose shooting board

With its long base and two-part fence, this jig can handle five different planing jobs.

¼-20 bolt, 2 in. long

Fence, 1½ in. thick by 2⅞ in. wide by 11¼ in. long

Low stop, ⅜ in. thick by ½ in. wide by 6½ in. long

Base, made from ½-in. plywood, 6½ in. wide by 30 in. long

Shallow rabbet for cleat

¼-20 T-nut

Vise cleat, 1½ in. sq. by 30 in. long

to make it, and demonstrate how I use it for all five tasks.

Simple to make

The base of the shooting board is made from ½-in. plywood. Beneath it is a hardwood cleat that runs the length of the base and fits your bench vise. On top is a two-part fence: A low, narrow stop is screwed into a dado and a tall, wide fence fits over the stop.

Start with the base. Cut a shallow rabbet in the bottom of the base along one edge. This will register the cleat and ensure that it's parallel to the base. Spread glue in the rabbet, clamp the cleat in place, and then drive in some brad nails.

After letting the glue dry, take the base to the tablesaw and cut a shallow dado at one end for the low stop. (Leave the blade height set for now. You'll use it again.) For a right-

hander like me, the dado should be at the left end of the base. If you and your bench are lefties, put it at the right end. Next, drill the counterbore and through-hole for the T-nut. This nut receives a bolt that helps hold the tall fence in place. Knock the T-nut into the hole. Fit the low stop into the dado and then screw it into place.

The fence, made from hardwood, now gets grooved on the bottom to fit over the low stop in the base. Cut the groove with the same setup used to cut the dado in the base. Then cut a slot parallel to the back edge of the fence for the bolt that threads into the T-nut. I cut the slot with my horizontal mortiser, but a handheld router and edge guide are just as effective.

Next, use the bandsaw to cut off the back corner of the fence at 45°. The angle doesn't need to be perfect, because you'll

Make the base. Plywood is a better choice than MDF, because it's more durable. Make sure to use a piece that's dead flat. The rabbet's short shoulder is tall enough to register the cleat parallel to the edge of the base, while the glue creates a strong bond that prevents the cleat from shifting in use.

Pop in some brads. They hold the cleat in place as the glue dries.

Cut a dado for the stop. It doesn't need to be deep—³⁄₁₆ in. works great. Locate it 2 in. or so from the end.

Insert a T-nut from below. After drilling a counterbore and a through-hole, hammer in the nut from the bottom.

Put the stop in the dado. Start wide and plane it down so that it just fits, then screw it down in the middle.

true it when you use the shooting board for miters.

Fit the fence onto the low stop and lock it down. Then check it for square, marking the high spots with a pencil. Take the fence off the base, and plane down those high spots. Reattach the fence and check for square again. Repeat until the fence is perfectly square to the base's edge.

That's it. The shooting board is ready for work.

Simple to use

Paired with a sharp No. 6 bench plane, this shooting board can do so much: trim end grain and miters, shoot edge grain, and plane face grain on boards that are thin or thick, wide or narrow. Whatever the task,

Add the fence. Used to trim both square end grain and miters, the fence is quick to reposition and easy to keep true. Groove the fence to fit the stop. Set the rip fence to cut a groove down the middle of the fence. The blade's height should be the same as it was for the dado in the base.

Miter the back corner. After cutting a slot for the bolt, clip the back corner of the fence at 45°.

Check for square. The fence is normally a bit out of square at this point. Look for high spots and mark them with pencil.

True the fence. Plane just the high spots at first and then take a full-length shaving.

90° setup

Zero-clearance fence. Set the fence just a hair over the base's edge. Rousseau does this with the bolt snug, tapping the fence's other end with a mallet (far left). Then plane the fence flush to the base's edge (left). This prevents tearout on the back edge of the workpiece.

5 ways to use the jig

What's better than a set of accurate and easy-to-make shooting boards? A single one that handles five planing jobs with no fuss.

1

Clean up end grain. Cleaning up end grain is a shooting board's basic function. Press the workpiece against the fence with just a bit overhanging the base. Take a pass, slide the workpiece out again. Take another pass. Repeat until the end is clean and square.

(Continued on next page)

Joint edges. With the end grain against the fence, you can also shoot long grain. Rousseau clamps the workpiece to the base to help stabilize it. Because breakout isn't a concern, the part can overhang the edge and fence.

Plane thin parts. After removing the fence, you can use the low stop for planing boards as thin as ³⁄₁₆ in. thick. The base provides a stable, flat planing platform.

A stop for wide boards. To face-plane wide boards, slide at least half the base off the bench and then clamp it in the vise. Set the workpiece against the end of the base and plane. Because the base is low, you won't clip it with the plane at the end of a stroke.

Trim miters. When shooting miters, there's always a danger that the plane will pull the workpiece forward as it cuts. The solution is to take smooth, easy passes. Thin shavings are better than heavy ones, too, because it takes less force to make them.

45° setup

Not slippery when wet. Before using the fence for miters, Rousseau spreads water on the bottom, which makes the fence and base grip each other a bit so the fence won't slip as you clamp it.

Clamp the fence. Set its angle with a combination square. Be sure the fence's back corner is in contact with the low stop. This will keep the fence from shifting backward under the force of planing.

the cleat on the bottom should be clamped in a vise.

The most common use for a shooting board is cleaning up and trimming end grain. For this, the tall fence should be locked in place with the bolt. I always set the fence so that it overhangs the edge of the base just a fuzz. I then use my plane to shoot it flush to the edge of the base, creating a zero-clearance fence that prevents tearout when you trim end grain.

Another way to use the shooting board is for shooting edge grain. There's nothing tricky about it. With the fence set to 90°, place the board's end grain against the fence, with the edge hanging over the base's edge. Plane the edge. You'll get it straight and square in no time.

The shooting board can also be used to plane face grain. For thin boards, I take off the fence and plane against the low stop. For face-planing wide boards, I slide the jig to the left so about half its length hangs off the end of the bench and then clamp it in the vise. This gives me more space along the front edge of the bench. Butt the board against the base and plane it.

Finally, with a quick adjustment, the jig excels at trimming miters. You remove the bolt, flip the fence over, and set it at 45° to the edge of the base with a combination square, making sure the back corner of the fence is against the low stop and the 45° face is overhanging a bit so you can plane it flush for zero clearance. Then clamp it down. I prefer this over a dedicated fence always set to 45°, because there's no guarantee a dedicated fence will remain at 45° through the seasons. With this jig, I can always quickly set it dead perfect.

4 Bench Jigs for Handplanes

NORMAN PIROLLO

Like many woodworkers, I began with hand tools but quickly progressed to using machines for almost every aspect of my work. A few years ago, as I developed my woodworking business, I decided there must be a less dusty and more peaceful way to make furniture. I took courses at a woodworking school whose philosophy was all about hand tools. This experience opened my eyes; you might say I became a born-again woodworker. Safety was also a factor in my transformation. For example, it can be dangerous to machine small parts on a tablesaw or bandsaw.

Now, instead of hearing the drone and whine of machines and breathing dust all day, I listen to classical music and sweep up shavings at the end of the day.

While I do use machinery sparingly, productivity remains the key to any business, so I've had to make my handplaning efficient without sacrificing quality. I use a series of jigs for different planing situations. The jigs have ¾-in.-dia. dowels that fit into dog holes in my workbench. If your bench doesn't have dog holes already, you need to drill only two or three because all the jigs are interchangeable. The jigs and techniques I'll describe are by no means new—handplanes have been used for centuries—but I've added my own modifications. One of these is that I'm left-handed, so you'll need to flip the plans if you're a righty.

Use a planing stop to go faster

Aside from efficiency, you get a better feel for the work when the board is held against a single plane stop rather than being pinched between two dogs.

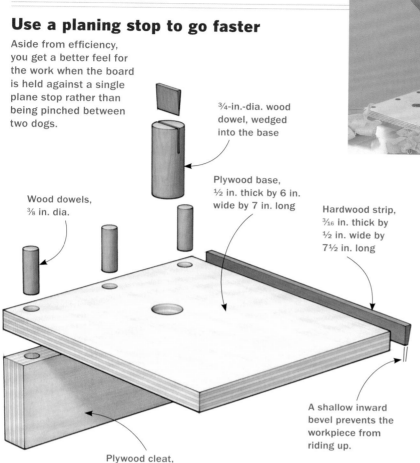

¾-in.-dia. wood dowel, wedged into the base

Wood dowels, ⅜ in. dia.

Plywood base, ½ in. thick by 6 in. wide by 7 in. long

Hardwood strip, ³⁄₁₆ in. thick by ½ in. wide by 7½ in. long

A shallow inward bevel prevents the workpiece from riding up.

Plywood cleat, ¾ in. thick by 2¼ in. wide by 6 in. long, hooks against the edge of the benchtop.

1. Planing stop

For face-planing boards at least ½ in. thick, I use a simple stop that is attached to the bench with a single dowel. To prevent the jig from pivoting in use, a cleat registers against the front edge of the bench.

After cutting out the two parts, clamp them together and place them on the workbench, centered over a dog hole. Insert a ¾-in.-dia. Forstner bit into the hole from the underside of the bench and use the spur to mark the location on the bottom of the jig base. Use the same bit to drill the hole on the drill press, and then use a ⅜-in.-dia. brad-point bit to drill three holes for the dowels that will connect the cleat.

Dowel stock varies fractionally in diameter; a slightly loose fit is fine in the dog hole, but you need a tight fit into the base of the

Locate the big dowel. Center the base over a dog hole. Use a ¾-in. Forstner bit to nick the underside of the base where you will drill.

Drill for the others. With a ⅜-in. brad-point bit, drill three holes at the front of the base for dowels that connect the cleat.

Attach the cleat. Insert the big dowel, ensure the base is square to the bench, then clamp on the cleat and extend the ⅜-in. dowel holes.

jig. To ensure a good fit, I saw a kerf into the top of the ¾-in. dowel. I apply glue and insert the dowel, then compress a hardwood wedge into the kerf using the jaws of a vise, which locks the dowel in place.

When the glue is dry, insert the base into the dog hole, clamp on the cleat, square the base to the edge of the bench, and extend the ⅜-in.-dia. holes into the cleat. Glue in the dowels and, when dry, plane everything flush with the base.

On the working edge of the stop, I glue a strip of hardwood with a shallow inward bevel on its face to keep boards from slipping upward. I apply a single coat of oil finish to my jigs for looks and protection, but this is optional.

2. Bird's-mouth stop

When edge-planing long boards, I employ a bird's-mouth stop. This attachment works remarkably well for holding a board on edge and is much faster than using a front vise, with or without a board jack.

Attached to the bench via two adjacent dog holes, this jig takes a bit more time to make than the last one, but the top two dowels give great rigidity and eliminate any tendency for rotation. Any board up to about 1½ in. thick can be inserted into the V-shaped slot in the jig and held in place with a small hardwood wedge on either side. The easiest way to make the wedges is to use the opening in the base as a template, cut the wedges on the bandsaw, and then clean them up with a handplane while holding them in a vise.

Edge-planing made easy. A bird's-mouth jig allows you to rest the whole length of a board on the bench while you edge-plane it. If held in a vise, only a part of the board is supported.

Wedges in a bird's mouth stop hold long boards on edge

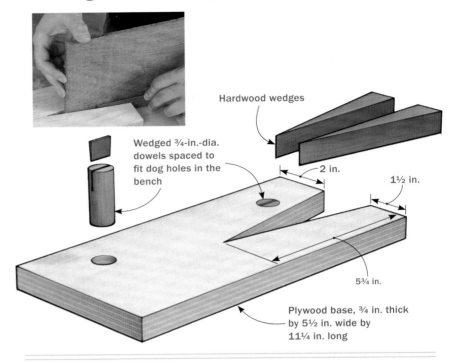

Hardwood wedges

Wedged ¾-in.-dia. dowels spaced to fit dog holes in the bench

2 in.

1½ in.

5¾ in.

Plywood base, ¾ in. thick by 5½ in. wide by 11¼ in. long

A flat surface. Even if your benchtop isn't flat, the plywood base of the planing board provides a flat surface to plane on.

The planing board is a multifunctional jig

Once you build this planing board, it is likely to become a permanent part of your bench.

Wedged ¾-in.-dia. dowels spaced to fit alternate benchdog holes

Opening is 1½ in. wide by 5¾ in. deep.

Bird's-mouth stop, plywood, ½ in. thick by 4½ in. wide by 8½ in. long

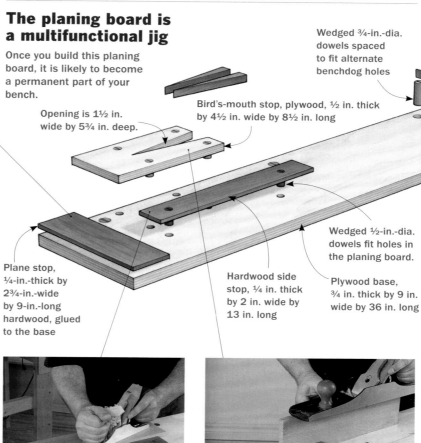

Plane stop, ¼-in.-thick by 2¾-in.-wide by 9-in.-long hardwood, glued to the base

Hardwood side stop, ¼ in. thick by 2 in. wide by 13 in. long

Wedged ½-in.-dia. dowels fit holes in the planing board.

Plywood base, ¾ in. thick by 9 in. wide by 36 in. long

Thin stock, no problem. When planing stock less than ¼ in. thick, add an auxiliary base of ⅛-in.-thick Masonite so the plane will clear the stop.

Side support. When you need to skew the plane or plane across the board, use the side stop to support the workpiece laterally.

There's more. Once you've planed the face of the board, use the bird's-mouth attachment to plane the board's edge.

3. Planing board

I reach for my planing board when working shorter or otherwise difficult workpieces. It combines a flat base with smaller versions of the first two jigs in this article.

The planing board has two advantages. It guarantees a flat surface to plane on, even if the benchtop isn't flat. Also, it allows me to plane thin, narrow stock. I add a base of ⅛-in.-thick Masonite to plane stock less than ¼ in. thick instead of installing a thinner plane stop.

If I need to skew the plane slightly to lower the cutting angle and slice through difficult grain, I add a removable side stop that plugs into the planing board using two ½-in.-dia. dowels. This provides lateral support.

For jointing the edges of boards, I attach a smaller version of the bird's-mouth stop. In this way I can plane the face and the edge grain of a short workpiece without removing the planing board.

Square and true. Place the board against the fence with the end fractionally beyond the end of the fence. Slide the plane past it, taking thin shavings until the end of the board is clean and perfectly square.

Basic shooting board planes ends square

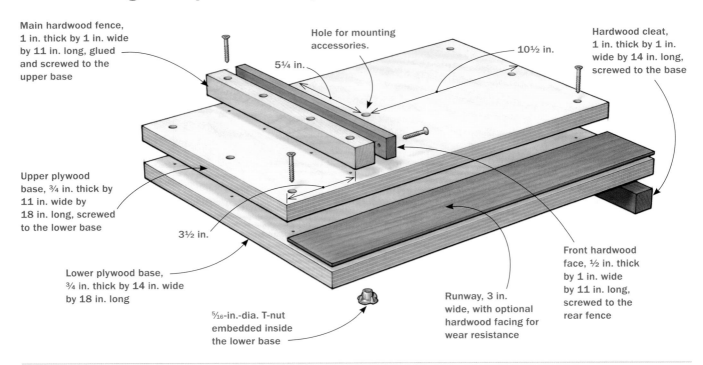

Main hardwood fence, 1 in. thick by 1 in. wide by 11 in. long, glued and screwed to the upper base

Hole for mounting accessories.

5¼ in.

10½ in.

Hardwood cleat, 1 in. thick by 1 in. wide by 14 in. long, screwed to the base

Upper plywood base, ¾ in. thick by 11 in. wide by 18 in. long, screwed to the lower base

3½ in.

Lower plywood base, ¾ in. thick by 14 in. wide by 18 in. long

⁵⁄₁₆-in.-dia. T-nut embedded inside the lower base

Runway, 3 in. wide, with optional hardwood facing for wear resistance

Front hardwood face, ½ in. thick by 1 in. wide by 11 in. long, screwed to the rear fence

4. Shooting board

When it comes to trimming the ends of boards, especially small ones, I turn to my shooting board. The jig, which hooks over the edge of the benchtop, consists of a base, a fence, and a runway for a handplane to glide along. The plane removes shavings in fine increments, leaving the board the correct length and the ends square and smooth, ready to be used in joinery.

The two-part fence, which supports the work and prevents tearout, must be exactly 90° to the runway and flush with the edge of the top base. The main fence is glued and screwed to the base, while the front face is screwed to the main fence so that it can be shimmed if needed. The best plane to use is a low-angle jack plane whose 37° cutting angle, long body, and large mass make it ideal for shaving end grain. Push the plane downward and toward the end of the workpiece with one hand, and use the other to secure the workpiece against the fence. This movement takes a little getting used to but soon becomes second nature.

A square fence is critical. If the front face of the fence isn't 90° to the runway, you can shim it.

Make a runway for the plane. The 3-in.-wide runway is formed by screwing the upper base to the lower base.

Trim the end. Before use, trim the fence flush with the edge of the top base. Clamp a piece of scrap to the fence to prevent tearout.

Two accessories for perfect miters

I recommend two easily installed attachments for this shooting board. The first is a triangular-shaped piece of plywood used to tune a flat, or frame, miter; the second is a larger block of wood with a face angled at 45°, used to trim a standing, or carcase, miter. Both attachments are held to the base using threaded rod that is screwed into a T-nut embedded in the underside of the jig. This group of easily constructed jigs leaves joints that surpass those left by a machine, and does it quicker.

Frame miters

Carcase miters

Frame miters

By adding a 45° plywood fence, you can use the shooting board to fine-tune parts for a mitered frame.

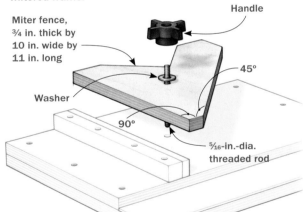

Miter fence, ¾ in. thick by 10 in. wide by 11 in. long

Handle

Washer

45°

90°

⁵⁄₁₆-in.-dia. threaded rod

Carcase miters

A second auxiliary fence allows you to trim carcase miters, leaving them at precisely 45° and free of saw marks.

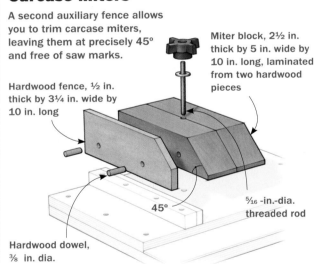

Miter block, 2½ in. thick by 5 in. wide by 10 in. long, laminated from two hardwood pieces

Hardwood fence, ½ in. thick by 3¼ in. wide by 10 in. long

45°

⁵⁄₁₆-in.-dia. threaded rod

Hardwood dowel, ⅜ in. dia.

Locate the hole from underneath. Hold the miter fence in position on the shooting board.

Check the angle. Make sure the fence is exactly 45° to the edge of the runway.

Laminated block. The large glue surface needs plenty of clamps to create enough pressure.

Quick change. The T-nut, threaded rod, and knob allow quick removal of both miter fences.

Making Sense of Vises

GARRETT HACK

A good bench vise is nearly as useful as a shop apprentice. On my bench I have a front vise and a large tail vise—I call them my right- and left-hand men. It's hard to imagine woodworking without them; they hold my work firmly so that I can concentrate fully on powering and controlling the tool I'm using.

In general, you'll find vises at two locations on a woodworker's bench: one on the long side of the bench, typically at the left-hand corner for right-handed woodworkers, and another on the short side at the opposite end.

The first, known variously as a side vise or front vise, matches the mental picture that most people have of a vise, with a movable jaw capturing work between it and the edge of the bench.

The second, called an end vise or tail vise, can clamp work like a front vise, but is more often used to hold boards flat on the bench, pinched between a pin or dog in the vise and another in one of the many holes along the benchtop. Together, these two vises can meet all of a woodworker's basic needs when it comes to holding work firmly and within reach.

Up front: a vise to clamp work vertically or on edge

A front vise, typically found on the bench's left-front corner, is ideal when you need to clamp a board to plane an edge, hold a chair leg while shaping it, or hold a board upright for sawing dovetails. The most common design is quite simple: a jaw of wood, or cast iron lined with wood, that moves with a single screw and a T-handle. The rest of the vise is mortised into the front edge of the bench. Mine opens about 10 in. and has about 4 in. of depth.

Many of the front vises on the market are fairly easy to fit to a benchtop. Look for one that has a large screw with well-cut Acme threads. These are the same square threads found on good clamps; they can smoothly deliver lots of force over a long life.

To hold long boards, wide panels, or doors securely on edge in a front vise, you need the added support of the deep front apron of the bench. Properly installed, the fixed half of the vise should be mortised into the bench so that the movable jaw clamps against the apron. This creates a great deal of stability, making it possible to clamp most boards on edge with no other support. For very long boards, just put one end in the front vise and rest the other on a short board clamped in the tail or end vise, much like a board jack on traditional benches. You can clamp a large tabletop vertically against the front edge of a bench, one end held in the front vise and the other held by a bar clamp across the bench.

A problem can arise, though, when clamping on just one side of the vise, such as when holding just the end of a much larger piece, clamping pieces vertically for laying out or sawing dovetails, or holding tapered or

Front vise

It typically occupies the left-front corner of the bench and is used to hold stock upright for sawing or for working edges.

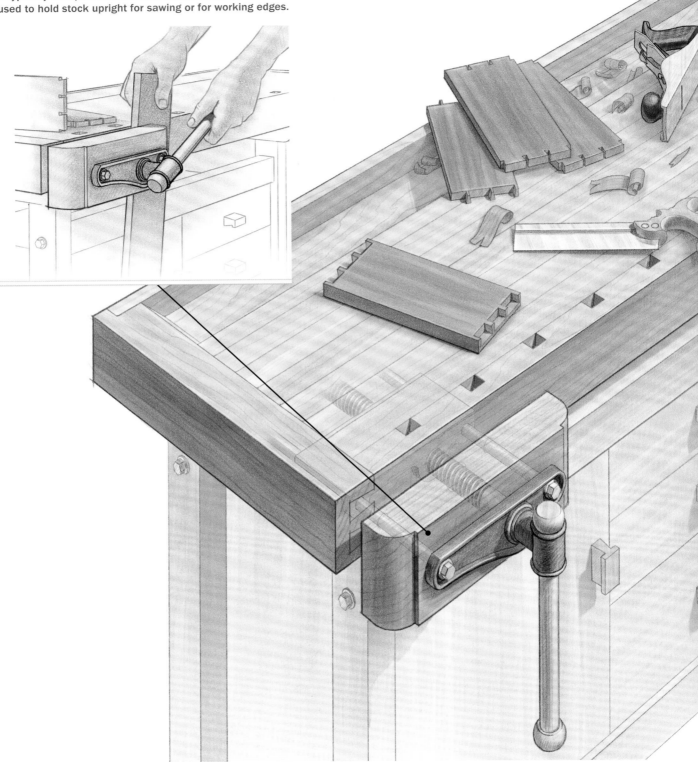

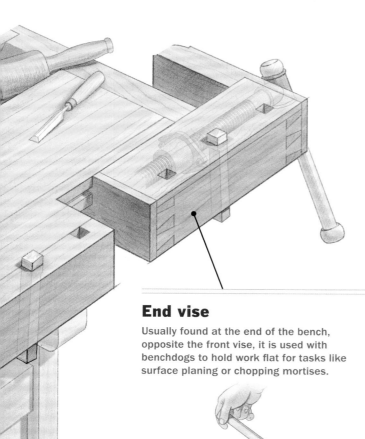

End vise

Usually found at the end of the bench, opposite the front vise, it is used with benchdogs to hold work flat for tasks like surface planing or chopping mortises.

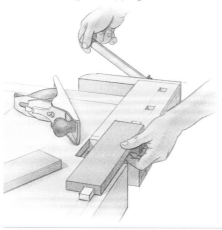

Front vises. Hold work vertically for sawing dovetails or planing end grain. A scrap piece of similar thickness, clamped in the opposite side of the vise, prevents the vise from racking.

Hold wide workpieces on edge. The vise screw prevents a wide piece from going all the way through the vise (right). A clamp seated in a dog hole provides extra support (above).

Types of front vise

Cast iron

The most popular front vise is cast iron. A steel rod or two keep the jaw aligned. Some also have a quick-action release for faster jaw adjustments.

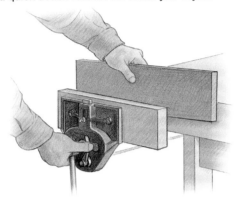

Wooden-jawed

A wooden-jawed vise operates like its cast-iron cousin. The movable jaw is typically made from the same material as the bench. Some models offer quick-release.

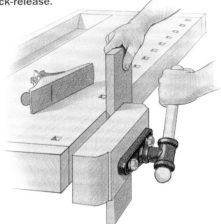

Arm Vise

An arm vise works well on wide boards. There are no screws or rods in the way. But the right-angled arm limits clamping force, which reduces the ability to clamp long boards horizontally.

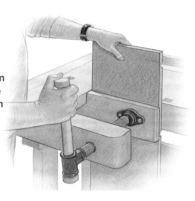

Build it yourself. Many companies sell the hardware for these vises. Look for a large screw with square-cut threads.

Patternmaker's vise

A patternmaker's vise can hold oddly shaped work at any angle. The vise body can pivot up and over the bench until the jaws are parallel to the benchtop. The jaws also can rotate 360° and angle toward one another for holding tapered work.

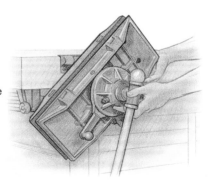

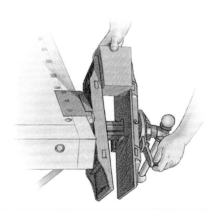

Secure long boards on edge. A block clamped in the tail vise supports the opposite end.

Steady a wide panel. A sawhorse provides support underneath, with the opposite end clamped to the bench apron.

oddly shaped pieces. When one side of the jaw is applying all the pressure—or trying to—it is very hard on the screw and any alignment rods, and can even distort them. One solution is to slip a block as thick as the workpiece into the other side of the jaw (use a wedge for odd shapes). This keeps the jaws parallel so you can apply all the pressure you need. Some bench manufacturers equip their front vises with a threaded stop that does the same job.

At the end: a vise to hold work flat

At the other end of the bench, you typically will find one of two distinct types of vises, known as end vises or tail vises. Their main purpose is to hold work flat on the surface of the bench.

A traditional tail vise, with one row of dog holes along the front edge of the bench and several more in the movable jaw, allows you to hold work flat over nearly the entire length of the bench. This is ideal for holding long boards to smooth a face, bead one edge, or hold a leg while chopping a mortise. You can also clamp across the grain to bevel a panel end or shape the skirt of a chest side. Be careful to apply only modest pressure to hold the work, or you will bow it up.

The tail vise is also great for holding long or odd pieces at any angle—there are no screws in the way and the hefty construction tends to prevent racking on odd shapes. Also, it can hold a workpiece at right angles to the bench edge, ideal for planing an end-grain edge, shooting a miter on a molding, or paring a tenon shoulder.

One drawback with this vise is that the large movable jaw can sag. A misaligned jaw makes it difficult to hold work flat on the benchtop. Avoid chopping or pounding over the movable jaw; it isn't as solid as the benchtop itself. Support the work as much as possible over the bench, with the least amount of jaw open. I keep small, square blocks handy to shim my work toward the bench or protect it from the dogs. I shouldn't have to say this, but never sit on your tail vise.

Another type of end vise—The other popular type of end vise looks and works like a front vise, except that the movable jaw is mounted to, and set parallel with, the end of the bench. If I had to outfit a bench with just one vise, it would be this type (see top drawing, p 215). My small traveling bench has an

An end vise holds work flat. Aligned with a row of dog holes, this vise has a wide capacity. It can hold smaller work and pieces nearly as large as the benchtop. It's ideal for smoothing a tabletop.

A secure grip for cross-grain work. The end vise allows you to clamp a panel across its width for tasks such as planing a bevel on the end.

For chopping, a spacer keeps the work off the vise jaw. The pounding could damage the vise. The best support is on the benchtop itself, right over a leg.

An end vise also handles awkward shapes. Pieces like this curved table apron can be held securely for scraping or other tasks.

old front vise mounted on one end in line with a row of dog holes.

Some end vises of this type have a jaw that spans the entire width of the bench. Equipped with a dog on each end of the jaw, and paired with a double row of dog holes down the front and back of the bench, this is a great system for holding wide parts flat on the benchtop. Several ready-made benches are built this way. Lee Valley also sells the necessary hardware for making the vise yourself.

Types of end vise

Cast iron

Same vise, different location. The cast-iron front vise also works well as an end vise—a smart solution if you have room or money for only one vise.

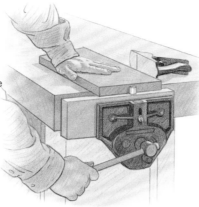

The guts. Tail-vise hardware comes with instructions for making the wood components.

Tail vise

The traditional end vise. The movable jaw is a thick section of the bench's front edge, about 18 in. long. Dog holes hold work flat on the surface. The jaws also can hold work at an angle.

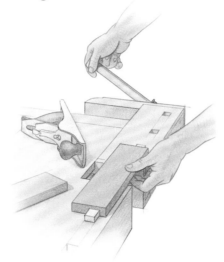

Full width

A modern variation spans the width of the bench. With two rows of dog holes, the wide jaw of this vise is ideal for holding wider panels.

Twin-screw

A twin-screw model can clamp wide stock vertically. A chain connects the two screws to prevent racking.

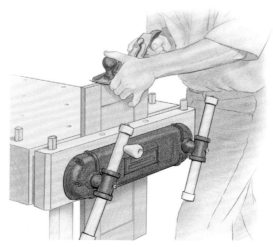

Metric Equivalents

INCHES	CENTIMETERS	MILLIMETERS	INCHES	CENTIMETERS	MILLIMETERS
⅛	0.3	3	13	33.0	330
¼	0.6	6	14	35.6	356
⅜	1.0	10	15	38.1	381
½	1.3	13	16	40.6	406
⅝	1.6	16	17	43.2	432
¾	1.9	19	18	45.7	457
⅞	2.2	22	19	48.3	483
1	2.5	25	20	50.8	508
1¼	3.2	32	21	53.3	533
1½	3.8	38	22	55.9	559
1¾	4.4	44	23	58.4	584
2	5.1	51	24	61	610
2½	6.4	64	25	63.5	635
3	7.6	76	26	66.0	660
3½	8.9	89	27	68.6	686
4	10.2	102	28	71.7	717
4½	11.4	114	29	73.7	737
5	12.7	127	30	76.2	762
6	15.2	152	31	78.7	787
7	17.8	178	32	81.3	813
8	20.3	203	33	83.8	838
9	22.9	229	34	86.4	864
10	25.4	254	35	88.9	889
11	27.9	279	36	91.4	914
12	30.5	305			

Contributors

Christian Becksvoort, *Fine Woodworking* contributing editor, is a professional furniture maker in New Gloucester, Maine.

Timothy Coleman is an award-winning furniture maker in Shelburne, Mass.

Barry NM Dima is *Fine Woodworking*'s associate editor.

Kelly J. Dunton is restoring his 100-year-old barn as a place for chickens, ducks, and cars, but he's reserving the second story for his woodworking shop.

Megan Fitzpatrick is a writer, teacher, and furniture maker in Cincinnati, Ohio.

Chris Gochnour is a *Fine Woodworking* contributing editor.

Garrett Hack, a professional furniture maker and woodworking instructor, is a *Fine Woordworking* contributing editor.

Matt Kenney was a *Fine Woodworking* special projects editor.

Steve Latta, *Fine Woodworking* contributing editor, teaches woodworking at Thaddeus Stevens College of Technology in Lancaster, Pa.

Mason McBrien is a woodworker in Mid-Coast Maine

Jeff Miller works wood in a converted post office in Chicago. He teaches woodworking there and around the country.

John Parkinson is a professional furniture maker in Durham, N.C.

Michael Pekovich is a woodworking teacher, author, and *Fine Woodworking* editor and creative director.

Norman Pirollo is the owner of Refined Edge Furniture Design in Ottawa, Ont., Canada.

Timothy Rousseau, of Appleton, Maine, is a professional furniture maker and instructor at the Center for Furniture Craftsmanship in Rockport, Maine.

Christopher Schwarz is a writer and furniture maker in Covington, Ky.

Bob Van Dyke is the founder and director of the Connecticut Valley School of Woodworking in Manchester, Conn.

John White is a former shop manager at *Fine Woodworking*.

Credits

All photos are courtesy of *Fine Woodworking* magazine © The Taunton Press, Inc. except as noted below. The articles in this book appeared in the following issues of *Fine Woodworking:*

pp. 4–9: Build Your First Workbench by Bob Van Dyke, issue 223. Photos by Steve Scott. Drawings by Vince Babak.

pp. 10–19: A Small, Sturdy Workbench by Matt Kenney, issue 258. Photos by Matt Kenney. Drawings by John Hartman.

pp. 20–30: Sturdy, Knock-Down Workbench by Barry NM Dima, issue 293. Photos by Barry NM Dima. Drawings by Christopher Mills.

pp. 31–38: Simple and Stout Workbench by Mason McBrien, issue 279. Photos by Barry NM Dima. Drawings by John Hartman.

pp. 39–51: Build a Stout Workbench by Chris Gochnour, issue 265. Photos by Matt Kenney. Drawings by Dan Thornton.

pp. 52–61: Shaker Workbench by Michael Pekovich & Matt Kenney, issue 251. Photos by Fine Woodworking staff. Drawings by John Hartman.

pp. 62–73: Modified Roubo Is the Ultimate Workbench by Jeff Miller, issue 230. Photos by Jonathan Binzen. Drawings by John Hartman.

pp. 74–83: Outfeed Table Doubles as a Workbench by Kelly J. Dunton, issue 249. Photos by Matt Kenney. Drawings by Kelly J. Dunton.

pp. 84–91: Don't Build a New Workbench by Christopher Schwarz, issue 283. Photos by Christopher Schwarz. Drawing by Kelly J. Dunton.

pp. 92–99: Rethinking the Workbench, issue 268. Photos provided by the contributors. Drawings by Christopher Mills.

pp. 100–103: Work at the Right Height by Christian Becksvoort, issue 265. Photos by Michael Pekovich.

pp. 104–112: Under-Bench Tool Storage by Christian Becksvoort, issue 258. Photos by Jonathan Binzen except for pp. 104-105 by Michael Pekovich. Drawings by Christopher Mills.

pp. 113–118: Mini Workbench Works Wonders by Steve Latta, issue 244. Photos by Ben Blackmar. Drawings by John Hartman.

pp. 119–128: The Wired Workbench by John White, issue 223. Photos by Matt Kenney. Drawings by John Hartman.

pp. 129–136: A Saw Bench Is a Versatile Addition to Your Shop by Megan Fitzpatrick, issue 281. Photos by Anissa Kapsales except for photo p. 129 and right photo p. 130 by Chris Schwarz. Drawings by Dan Thornton.

pp. 137–145: 6 Essential Bench Jigs by Michael Pekovich, issue 258. Photos by Rachel Barclay except for the jig photos p. 137 and 138 by Michael Pekovich. Drawings by Dan Thornton.

pp. 146–151: Extra Help for Holding Work by Chris Gochnour, issue 266. Photos by Matt Kenney.

pp. 152–157: Make Short Work of Small Parts by Matt Kenny, issue 214. Photos by Patrick McCombe. Drawings by Vince Babak.

pp. 158–163: Get a Grip on Your Work by John Parkinson, issue 258. Photos by Matt Kenney.

pp. 164–170: Clever Clamping Tricks by Timothy Coleman, issue 261. Photos by Jonathan Binzen except for photo p. 164–165 by John Tetreault. Left drawing p. 166 by Chris Mills; right drawing p. 166 by Michael Gellatly.

pp. 171–175: These Puppies Have Bite by Timothy Coleman, issue 253. Photos by Thomas McKenna. Drawings by Vince Babak.

pp. 176–183: The Versatile Wedge by Bob Van Dyke, issue 249. Photos by Ben Blackmar.

pp. 184–194: All-in-One Workstation for Dovetails by Michael Pekovich, issue 282. Photos by Rachel Barclay. Drawings by Dan Thornton.

pp. 195–201: A Shooting Board that Handles Five Jobs by Timothy Rousseau, issue 267. Photos by Matt Kenney. Drawings by Dan Thornton.

pp. 202–208: 4 Bench Jigs for Handplanes by Norman Pirollo, issue 202. Photos by Mark Schofield except for bottom left photo p. 203 by Norman Pirollo. Drawings by Christopher Mills.

pp. 209–215: Making Sense of Vises by Garrett Hack, issue 191. Photos by Steve Scott. Drawings by John Hartman.

Index

A

Arms vise, 212
Auxiliary benches, 100–101, 103, 113–18

B

Bar clamps, 90, 91
Benchcrafted Glide Leg Vise and Tail Vise, 63–66
Benchdogs, dog holes, and dog boards
  bench puppies, 171–75
  dado head for cutting, 44–45
  DIY benchdogs, 98
  knock-down workbench, 22, 30
  minibench, 114, 115
  modified Roubo workbench, 65, 66, 67, 68, 71
  securing a board for planing with, 39, 42–43
  simple, solid workbench, 32, 33, 35, 38
  stout workbench, 39, 42–43, 44–45, 46, 49–51
  wired workbench, 121, 124, 125–28
  workbench in a weekend, 7, 9
Benchtop benches, 100–101, 103, 113–18
Bird's-mouth stop, 204, 205
Black Bear Forge, 160
Board jack, 53, 61
Box for hand-tool operations, 93–94

C

Cam clamps, 165–66, 169–70
Carver's clamp, 96
Cast-iron vise, 19, 114, 115–16, 212, 215
Cauls, L-shaped, 148, 149
Center for Furniture Craftsmanship, 31, 195
Clamps
  bar clamps, 90, 91
  cam clamps, 165–66, 169–70
  carver's clamp, 96
  hand-screw clamps, 66, 68, 91, 150, 164–70

holding work with, 150
  toggle clamps, 187, 188, 189–91, 192
  tricks for using, 164–70
  as vise alternatives, 90–91
Clouterie Rivierre nails, 135
College os the Redwoods, 171
Crochet (hook), 90
Cuff jig, 68, 69

D

Dado set/dadoes
  cutting dog holes, 44–45
  cutting joints, 5, 7, 74, 77, 78, 79
  plywood case for storage, 103, 109–11
Doe's foot, 89–90
Dovetails
  box for hand-tool operations, 93–94
  clamps as vise alternative for cutting, 90, 91
  half-blind, 194
  knock-down workbench, 25, 26–27
  modified Roubo workbench, 65, 69–70
  routing, 191–94
  stout workbench, 49–50
  work stand for, 184–94
Drawbore pegs, 57, 58–59, 78–79, 80
Drawers
  dividers for organizing, 95
  Shaker workbench, 54, 60–61
  wood drawers and flush-mount pulls, 107, 109, 111–12
Dumbbell bars, 94–95
Dust collection system, 119, 120, 121–23, 125

E

Eclipse quick-release vise, 115–16
Electric power source for workbenches, 119, 120
End vise, 209, 211, 213–15

F

Festool Dominoes, 45, 50

Forstner bit, 16, 17, 47, 48, 72, 78
Front vise, 147–49, 209–10, 211, 212–13
Full-width vise, 213–14, 215

G

Glue-ups and wedges, 178, 179, 180–81
Glulam beam (laminated beam), 92–93
Gramercy Tools holdfasts, 89, 160

H

Hamilton Marine, 109, 111
Hancock Shaker Village, 53
Hand-screw clamps, 66, 68, 91, 150, 164–70
Height of workbenches, 100–103
  benchtop bench to raise work surface, 100–101, 103
  minibench to raise work surface, 113–18
  platform to lower work surface, 100, 101–2
  wired workbench, 119–28
Holdfasts
  holes in benchtop for using, 161–63
  recommendations for, 89, 160
  uses for and how to use, 88–91, 146–47, 149–51, 159–63
Hook (crochet), 90

I

I-beam legs, 114, 116–18
Improvements to existing workbench, 84–91
  legs as clamping surfaces, 86, 87
  sliding, elimination of, 85
  sway and wobble, ending, 84–85
  vises, improving grip of, 86–87
  workholding with no end vise, 87–91

J

Jigs, 137–45, 202–8
  bird's-mouth stop, 204, 205
  narrow parts, stop for, 137, 140
  parallel supports holding jig, 146, 149, 151
  planing board, 205
  planing stops, 87–90, 137–43, 153–54, 203–4
  saw block for small, thin parts, 138, 145
  saw hooks, 137–38, 144–45, 153, 154–55
  shooting board, 138, 141–43, 153, 155–57, 195–201, 206–8
  small parts, stop for, 137, 143
  t-stop, 137, 139
Joinery
  dadoes and cutting joints on tablesaw, 5, 7, 74, 77, 78, 79
  interlocking joinery, 10–19
  laminated joinery, 25–26
  saw bench construction, 130–33
  See also Mortise-and-tenon joints
Jointer, workbench as, 97

K

Knock-down workbench, 20–30
  dog holes, 22, 30
  laminated joinery, 25–26
  leg vise and hardware, 22, 23, 28, 29–30
  wood for, 24–25

L

Laminated beam (glulam beam), 92–93
Lee Valley, 214
Leg vise and hardware, 22, 23, 28, 29–30, 62, 63–66, 70, 72, 73
Lie-Nielsen Toolworks, 160

M

Metal face vise, 42–43
Metal scoop, 99
Metric equivalents, 216

Ming dynasty furniture, 10, 11
Minibenches, 100–101, 103, 113–18
Minwax High Glass Polyurethane, 9
Miters, making perfect, 138, 141, 142, 143, 144, 157, 198, 200, 201, 208
Modified Roubo workbench, 62–73
   leg vise, 62, 63–66, 70, 72, 73
   top design and construction, 63, 64–65, 66–70
   top planing and flattening, 72–73
   wagon vise, 62, 63–66, 71
Moravian workbench, 20
Mortise-and-tenon joints
   box for hand-tool operations, 93–94
   cutting tenons, 12–16, 77, 79
   double tenons, 12
   drawbore pegs, 57, 58–59, 78–79, 80
   outfeed table, 74–79
   Shaker workbench, 53–59
   small, stable workbench, 10–19
   stopped mortises, 25–26
Moxon vise, 93, 94

N

Narrow parts, stop, 137, 140

O

Offerman's sled and Nick Offerman, 97
Oneida Dust Deputy, 119, 120, 121–23, 125
Outfeed table, 74–83
   base construction and assembly, 74–79, 80
   top design and construction, 74, 79–80, 81, 83
   vise, 74, 76, 80, 82–83

P

Patternmaker's vise, 212
Pilot holes, 135
Pivot jaw for tapered work, 116
Planing
   bench jigs, 137–45, 202–8

securing a board with benchdogs, 39, 42–43
Planing board, 205
Planing stops, 87–90, 137–43, 153–54, 203–4
Platform to lower work surface, 100, 101–2
Power tools, workbench designed for, 119–28
Puppies, bench, 171–75

R

Roubo, André Jacob, 64
Roubo benches, 20
   See also Modified Roubo workbench
Routers
   dovetailing with, 191–94
   hand-screw clamp use with, 168
   router sled and workbench as jointer, 97

S

Saw benches, 129–36
   height of, 135–36
   how to use, 130
Saw hooks, 137–38, 144–45, 153, 154–55
Scoop, metal, 99
Shaker workbench, 52–61
   base construction and finish, 53–59
   board jack, 53, 61
   drawbore pegs, 58–59
   drawer box and drawers, 54, 60–61
   top design and construction, 59, 61
Shooting board, 138, 141–43, 153, 155–57, 195–201, 206–8
Shop vacuum, 119, 120, 121–23, 125
Simple, solid workbench, 31–38
   materials for, 31–34
   vise, 32, 34–35, 37
Small, stable workbench, 10–19
   assembly order, 17–18
   interlocking joinery, 10–19
Small parts, stop, 137, 143
Storage
   under-bench tool storage, 104–12
   drawers and drawer pulls, 107, 109, 111–12
   layout tips for tools, 108

Shaker workbench, 52–61
Stout workbench, 39–51
   benchtop, 42–45
   tail vise, 42–43, 46–51
Switzer, John, 160

T

Tablesaw
   cutting dog holes, 44–45
   cutting joints on, 5, 7, 74, 77, 78, 79
Tail vise, 42–43, 46–51, 65, 147–49, 171, 172, 209, 213, 215
Tan, Eric, 10
Toggle clamps, 187, 188, 189–91, 192
T-stop, 137, 139
Twin-screw vise, 42–43, 215

V

Vacuum and dust collection system, 119, 120, 121–23, 125
Van Dyke, Bob, 187
V-blocks, 140
Veritas Fast-Action Hold-Down, 151
Veritas Quick-Release Front Vise, 41
Veritas Wonder Pup and Brass Bench Dog, 33, 35, 38
Vises
   arms vise, 212
   carver's clamp use with workbench vise, 96
   cast-iron vise, 19, 74, 76, 80, 82–83, 114, 115–16, 212, 215
   end vise, 209, 211, 213–15
   front vise, 147–49, 209–10, 211, 212–13
   full-width vise, 213–14, 215
   grip of, improvement of, 86–87
   holding work with, 146–49
   leg vise and hardware, 22, 23, 28, 29–30, 62, 63–66, 70, 72, 73
   metal face vise, 42–43
   Moxon vise, 93, 94
   patternmaker's vise, 212
   simple, solid workbench, 32, 34–35, 37
   tail vise, 42–43, 46–51, 65, 147–49, 171, 172, 209, 213, 215
   twin-screw vise, 42–43, 215

wagon vise, 42–43, 62, 63–66, 71
wedges to eliminate racking, 147
wooden-jawed vise, 212
workbench in a weekend, 4, 6, 9

W

Wagon vise, 42–43, 62, 63–66, 71
Wedges
   how to make, 177, 178–80
   racking elimination with, 147
   uses for and how to use, 176–83
White Chapel, 111
Wired workbench, 119–28
   electric power source for, 119, 120
   hose and cord management, 120, 128
   top design and construction, 120, 121, 124, 125–28
   vacuum and dust collection system, 119, 120, 121–23, 125
Wooden-jawed vise, 212
Wood/materials
   simple, solid workbench, 31–34
   top materials, 6, 7–8, 114–15
   using a saw bench to cut and support, 130
   wood for base, 5
   wood for sturdy, knock-down workbench, 24–25
Woodriver Large End Vise Slide, 41
Workbenches
   cost to build, 4
   durability of building own, 4–5
   price to buy, 4
   properties of good, 4
Workbench in a weekend, 4–9
   top materials and construction, 6, 7–8
   vise, 4, 6, 9